∞

The House of the Virgin Mary

Godfrey E. Phillips

The House of the Virgin Mary

The Miraculous Story of Its Journey
from Nazareth to a Hillside in Italy

SOPHIA INSTITUTE PRESS
Manchester, New Hampshire

The House of the Virgin Mary was originally published under the title *Loreto and the Holy House: Its History Drawn from Authentic Sources* (London: R. and T. Washbourne, 1917). The 1917 edition from which this new work is derived contained a number of anomalies and not a few errors of detail about the sources of the readings contained in it. In this new 2017 edition we have sought, where possible, to remedy those deficiencies. We apologize for any new problems our efforts may have introduced into this work.

Printed in the United States of America. All rights reserved.

Cover design by Coronation Media.

On the cover: public-domain, anonymous, sixteenth-century painting, *Die Überführung des Hauses der Maria nach Loreto*.

Sophia Institute Press
Box 5284, Manchester, NH 03108
1-800-888-9344

www.SophiaInstitute.com

Sophia Institute Press® is a registered trademark of Sophia Institute.

Library of Congress Cataloging-in-Publication Data

Names: Phillips, Godfrey E. (Godfrey Edward), 1878-1963, author.
Title: The house of the Virgin Mary : the miraculous story of its journey
   from Nazareth to a hillside in Italy / Rev. Godfrey E. Phillips.
Other titles: Loreto and the Holy House
Description: Manchester, New Hampshire : Sophia Institute Press, 2017. | "The
   House of the Virgin Mary was originally published under the title Loreto
   and the Holy House: Its History Drawn from Authentic Sources (London: R.
   and T. Washbourne, 1917)." | Includes bibliographical references.
Identifiers: LCCN 2017015757 | ISBN 9781622824489 (pbk. : alk. paper)
Subjects: LCSH: Mary, Blessed Virgin, Saint—Shrines—Italy—Loreto. | Santa
   Casa (Loreto, Italy) | Loreto (Italy)—Buildings, structures, etc.
Classification: LCC BX2321.L7 P49 2017 | DDC 263/.04245671—dc23 LC
record available at https://lccn.loc.gov/2017015757

First printing

*To the Right Reverend Father in Christ
Richard, Lord Bishop of Middlesbrough,
by whose side the writer has been privileged to kneel
within the sacred walls that once were
the earthly home of Jesus, Mary, and Joseph*

Contents

∞

Preface

In reply to a petition made to him by the bishops of the Province of Piceno, in which Loreto stands, our Holy Father Pope Benedict XV has issued a decree, dated April 12, 1916, ordering the Feast of the Translation of the Holy House to be henceforth observed each year, on the 10th of December, in all the dioceses and religious congregations of Italy and the adjacent isles. Moreover, by the same decree he grants permission for the extending of the festival to all other dioceses and religious congregations, on its being applied for by the ordinaries.

The Pontiff expressly grounds the granting of this favor on the acknowledged preeminence of the Loreto Sanctuary, it being, as the preamble states, "the House itself — translated from Palestine by the ministry of Angels — in which was born the Blessed Virgin Mary, and in which the Word was made flesh."[1]

In view of this decisive pronouncement of the reigning Pontiff as to the peculiar sanctity of the Loreto Shrine, it is hoped that the following account of that peculiarly sacred shrine and of its wondrous history, on which the writer has been engaged

---

[1]   *Acta Apostolicae Sedes* (Cittá del Vaticano, 1916), June 7, 1916, 179.

for several years, will be welcomed by many, and especially by those to whom the attacks of critics on the Holy House have given pain. The groundlessness of those attacks, and the solidity of the foundation on which the Loreto tradition rests, are here, he trusts, made plain.

It was a special encouragement to him in his pursuance of the work to receive, through his superior, the blessing on it of the late saintly Pope Pius X, a few weeks before his death.

In obedience to the decrees of Pope Urban VIII, he unreservedly submits what he has written to the judgment of the Holy See, especially with reference to the mentioning of any occurrence as miraculous.

∞

The House of the Virgin Mary

Chapter 1

∞

A Catholic's Attitude toward Loreto

We know not how better to open the subject of the following
pages than by setting before the reader the following extracts
from two letters of Cardinal Newman, which were addressed by
him in January 1848 to Henry Wilberforce, immediately after
his own return from Rome, where he had been ordained a priest
and had become an Oratorian.

> What took us to Bologna [wrote the future Cardinal] was
> that we went round by Loreto. We went there to get the
> Blessed Virgin's blessing on us. I have ever been under her
> shadow, if I may say it. My College was St. Mary's and my
> Church; and when I went to Littlemore, there, by my own
> previous disposition, Our Blessed Lady was waiting for me.

> I went to Loreto with a simple faith, believing what I still
> more believed when I saw it. I have no doubt now. If you
> ask me why I believe, it is because *everyone* believes it at
> Rome; cautious as they are and skeptical about some other
> things. I believe it, then, as I believe that there is a new
> planet called Neptune or that chloroform destroys the
> sense of pain. *I have no antecedent difficulty in the matter.*

He who floated the Ark on the surges of a world-wide sea and enclosed in it all living things, who has hidden the terrestrial paradise, who said that faith might move mountains, who sustained thousands for forty years in a sterile wilderness, who transported Elias and keeps him hidden till the end, could do this wonder also. And in matter of fact we see all other records of our Lord and His Saints gathered up in the heart of Christendom from the ends of the earth as Paganism encroached on it (i.e., His relics). St. Augustine leaves Hippo, the prophet Samuel and St. Stephen leave Jerusalem, the crib in which our Lord lay leaves Bethlehem with St. Jerome, the Cross is dug up, St. Athanasius goes to Venice. In short, I feel no *difficulty* in believing it, though it may be often difficult to *realize*.[2]

Such, then, was Cardinal Newman's attitude with reference to the belief in the miraculous translation of the Holy House, and in that same attitude, we are assured, did he continue to the end.[3]

It is true, indeed, that his biographer has thought well to append to the letters above quoted a note to the effect that when they were written "the recent criticism as to the history of the Holy House was unknown." Many, however, we feel sure, will agree with us in thinking that, in thus following the Catholic instinct that he had imbibed so strongly with the Faith, and in quietly accepting the pronouncements of the Pontiffs, Newman was really following much safer guidance than any that the

---

[2] Wilfrid Ward, *The Life of John Henry, Cardinal Newman: Based on His Private Journals and Correspondence*, 2 vols., vol. 1 (New York: Longmans, Green, 1912), 193, 198.

[3] Edward Bellasis, "Jottings about Cardinal Newman," *Month* (1913).

modern criticism could have offered. Though strongly opposed to exaggerated ways of speaking on the subject, it was the cardinal's belief, as his same biographer admits, "that the *pietas fidei* should prompt to internal submission beyond the sphere covered by strictly infallible decisions,"[4] and it must indeed be evident that our belief in God's guidance of the Holy See cannot be restricted simply to occasions as comparatively rare as those indicated in the Vatican Decree.

When, therefore, in a case such as that before us we find Pontiff after Pontiff encouraging in every way the belief in the miraculous translation—while the same belief, moreover, has been rapturously adopted by a host of saints, including even Doctors of the Church—it seems impossible to think that an error could have been allowed by God to receive such authoritative sanction.

On this point the following passage may usefully be quoted from a work, too little known, of the late learned Dr. Northcote:

> Although it is quite true that a belief in the identity of the Holy House of Loreto with that in which the Incarnation was accomplished, and its miraculous translation from Galilee to Italy, is no article of the faith, and a man may deny it, if he will, without thereby becoming a heretic, nevertheless it would be well for anyone who is tempted to do so to realize what he is doing. He is assuming that he is more intelligent than the great body of the faithful who for centuries have venerated this sanctuary and have regarded its history as true. He is assuming that he is more sagacious than the Saints,

---

[4]   Ward, *Life of Newman*, vol. 2, 227.

wiser than the Supreme Pontiffs who have rendered such magnificent testimonies to the truth of its history, and more prudent than the Sacred Congregation of Rites who have approved the office of the translation. Perhaps, also, it would be well for him to weigh the full significance of the following remarks, written by a very bitter enemy when examining this very subject: "There are individuals in the Roman Church who look upon certain parts of their system as matters in which they are free to please themselves; but whether in consequence or not, they are certainly none of the holiest.... We have discovered that belief and disbelief in the story of the Holy House amongst Roman Catholics go hand in hand respectively with ardent piety and indifferentism" (*Christian Remembrancer*, No. 84. N. S.). In other words, a man cannot throw off the spirit of dutifulness and submission to authority from a profound conviction of his own superior knowledge without suffering spiritual loss.[5]

As to the continuous approval bestowed on the Loreto tradition by the Sovereign Pontiffs, the following summary of their action with regard to it is taken from the same work of Dr. Northcote:

Of the sixty-five Popes who have filled the Chair of Peter since the miraculous translation took place, forty-four have in one way or other given their sanction to the story ... whilst of the twenty-one who do not happen to have spoken on the subject, seven lived before the return of

[5] J. Spencer Northcote, *Celebrated Sanctuaries of the Madonna* (London: Longmans, Green, 1868), 102.

the Popes from Avignon (where, of course, it was impossible that they should have had so accurate a knowledge of what was going on in Italy), and seven others reigned for a few weeks or months.[6]

Since the above was written, the two Pontiffs who have followed have each of them expressed their marked approval of the Loreto tradition. Under the first of these — the singularly enlightened Leo XIII — took place the sixth centenary of the arrival of the Holy House in Italy, and on occasion of it Pope Leo issued an encyclical, in which, without one word of hesitation, he reaffirmed the miraculous translation of it, inviting all the faithful to take part in the celebration of it, and granting a Jubilee indulgence to those who visited Loreto.

In various ways also our late Holy Father Pope Pius X openly manifested his belief in the tradition, and his great displeasure at the attacks made recently upon it.[7] It will be seen, I think, as we proceed, that these attacks have for their basis no fresh discovery disproving the tradition and are rested either upon grounds that are purely negative, such as the asserted absence of contemporary

---

[6] Ibid., 99.

[7] In reply to an enquiry about an informal permission for the publication of his work against Loreto, obtained by M. Chevalier from the Master of the Sacred Palaces, Pope Pius X directed Cardinal Merry del Val, his secretary of state, to write as follows: "As to M. Chevalier's recent publication, His Holiness was not at all pleased at the action of the Father Master of the Sacred Palaces. And in as much as he makes no mystery to anyone as to his displeasure at it, His Holiness desires that I should thus plainly declare it to you." Quoted from the *Annali della Santa Casa* for January 1907, by Rev. Alfonso di Gesu, *Oppositori e diffensori*, 181.

documents, or on unwarrantable accusations against those, by whom the tradition has been transmitted, of undue credulity, if not of actual imposture.

Disregarding, however, these objections for the moment, let us first see what it is that is now shown to the pilgrim to Loreto; and what is the story of the Holy House and its miraculous translation, which has been handed down by its historians.

Chapter 2

∞

What the Pilgrim to Loreto Sees

The following description of the Holy House, as it is seen at the present day by the pilgrim to Loreto, is borrowed from a work, now unfortunately out of print, called *Loreto and Nazareth* by the late Father William Anthony Hutchison of the London Oratory, who died while it was passing through the press in 1863. The three sanctuaries of Nazareth, Loreto, and Tersatto had each in turn been visited by him (the first two more than once), and everything had been examined by him carefully and leisurely upon the spot.

The following is his description of Loreto:

> On a hillside, on the east coast of Italy, at a distance of about three miles from the sea, and eighteen miles south of Ancona, stands the city of Loreto. On the summit of the hill, towering far above the surrounding buildings rises the magnificent cathedral church, with its great dome and campanile. Unlike any other church, it seems to have something of the nature of a castle, owing to the fortifications with which it is provided, in order to repel the attacks of pirates, who might seek to plunder the sanctuary which the church contains.

9

The House of the Virgin Mary

The dome of the great Loreto cathedral built over the Holy House, and its castle-like walls built to repel pirates

From its great height and from its position it may be seen, and the music of its bells is often heard, at a considerable distance out at sea.

On entering the church, there is seen beneath the dome a singular rectangular edifice, of no great height, constructed apparently of white marble, and richly adorned with statues and sculpture.

On entering this building, the contrast between the poverty of the interior — at least as far as the walls are concerned — and the richness of the marble exterior is most astonishing. The walls, as seen from the interior, are the plain, rough walls of a cottage, and evidently of great antiquity.

Toward the eastern end of the house, but at some little distance from the east wall, stands an altar, with

*The Holy House encased in marble
beneath the dome of the cathedral*

*The interior of the Holy House with the statue
of the Virgin and Child behind the altar*

The statue of the Virgin and Child

an altar-screen of pillars and arches, which divides the house into two unequal parts.

Behind the altar, in a niche in the east wall, is an image of Our Lady and Child. It is said to be of olive wood, and partly from the nature of the wood, and partly from age, and from the constant smoke of the lamps, which are ever burning before it, it has become perfectly black. Both the Virgin and Child wear on their heads precious crowns of gold, and the figure is clothed in a rich robe, adorned with brilliants and jewels. This is the famous image of Our Lady of Loreto.

On all sides of the house are suspended silver lamps, which are continually burning; and the contrast between

Sketch of the north wall of the Holy House

the richness of these lamps, and the roughness and poverty of the walls, is as striking as that already spoken of
between the interior and the magnificent marble exterior.

The peculiar hush and stillness, broken only by the
occasional clinking of a rosary, which is so characteristic
of an Italian sanctuary, may be especially observed here.
Yet the house is usually full of people on their knees praying to the Madonna, and as they leave they may generally
be seen affectionately kissing the ancient walls. There is
something in the aspect of the building which of itself
moves one to devotion; and this effect is intensified when
the mind dwells upon the various mysteries of which these
walls have been the witnesses.

Those who have had the happiness of visiting Loreto
will, I think, agree in saying that the moments spent in
the Holy House were among the happiest of their lives;
and if they only spent the time aright, they must have
arisen from their knees with the conviction common to

Sketch of the west wall of the Holy House

all the faithful who have visited it: "This is no other but the house of God, and the gate of Heaven."

This strange building, then, under the dome of the great church, is the Holy House of Loreto.[8]

To this description of the Holy House by Father Hutchison it will be convenient here to add a translation of the inscription, which, for the instruction of the pilgrims, was engraved by order of Pope Clement VIII upon the eastern end of the marble wall that encases the Holy House. Placed there by the Pontiff, as it was, expressly to inform the pilgrim of the facts, it is a clear and

[8] William Antony Hutchison, *Loreto and Nazareth: Two Lectures, Containing the Results of Personal Investigation of the Two Sanctuaries* (London: E. Dillon, 1863).

Sketch of the south wall of the Holy House

authoritative proof of the Holy See's acceptance of the miracle of the translation.

Inscription on the Marble Wall Enclosing the Holy House

Christian traveler, whom piety or vow has conducted hither, thou beholdest the holy Loreto House, renowned throughout the world for its divine mysteries and glorious miracles. Here the Most Holy Mary, Mother of God, was born; here she was saluted by the Angel; here the Eternal Word of God was made flesh. Angels transferred this habitation first from Palestine to Tersatto in Illyria, in the year of salvation 1291, Nicholas IV being then Sovereign Pontiff. Three years afterwards, in the commencement of the pontificate of Boniface VIII, it was transferred into Picenum, near to Recanati city, and placed by the ministry of Angels in the wood of this hill; where, having changed its place three times within the space of a year, it at length rested by God's will three hundred years ago. From that time, this Holy House has been held in great veneration among all nations, the admiration of the neighboring people being excited by so extraordinary an event, and the fame of the miracles wrought in it having been spread far and wide. Its walls, with no foundations to support them, remain whole and stable after so many ages. Pope Clement VII enclosed it within a marble casement in the year of our Lord 1534.

The Sovereign Pontiff Clement VIII ordered this brief account of the wonderful Translation to be engraved upon this stone in the year 1595. Anthony Maria Gallus, Cardinal Priest of the Holy Roman Church, and Bishop of Osimo, Protector of the Holy House, caused it to be done. Do thou, pious pilgrim, here devoutly venerate the Queen of Angels and Mother of Grace, that through her merits and intercession thou mayest obtain from her most loving Son, who is the author of life, pardon of thy sins, health of body, and eternal joys.

Within the Holy House itself a briefer inscription, set in letters of gold upon the reredos of the altar, and placed there, it seems, by authority of Pope Clement VII, by whom the altar was moved into its present position, again reminds the pilgrim of the great mystery accomplished within those very walls:

Hic Verbum Caro Factum Est Et Habitavit In Nobis.

We must now endeavor to trace the history of the Holy House from the time when it was the habitation of the Holy Family at Nazareth to its miraculous translation to Loreto.

Chapter 3

∞

The Holy House before Its Translation

We must endeavor first, as far as existing documents will allow us, to trace the history of the Holy House during the long period that preceded its translation into Europe—while it still occupied its original position in the little town of Galilee, where it had been the home of Our Blessed Lady and St. Joseph, and even of Our Blessed Lord Himself.

The site on which it stood at Nazareth is now shown in a crypt beneath the Church of the Annunciation, which was built over the sacred spot by the Franciscans who had charge of it in 1730. On every side around the present church are to be seen the ruins of the larger and more magnificent basilica erected there by the Crusaders, but demolished by the Saracens in 1263; while recent excavations made beneath the pavement of it have brought to light remains of a still more ancient church built there, according to tradition, by St. Helen.[9]

The tradition that the first church built over the scene of the Annunciation owed its origin to St. Helen is confirmed by what we know of that holy empress from St. Paulinus of Nola, who

---

[9] Barnabé Meisterman, *Nouveau Guide de Terre Sainte* (Paris, Procure Généraledu Clergé, 1907), 368.

speaks of her, as having erected basilicas over all the places in which had been accomplished "the mysteries of the Incarnation, Passion, Resurrection, and Ascension,"[10] and it was, of course, in Our Lady's house at Nazareth that the Incarnation of our Lord had taken place. Moreover, the authority of St. Paulinus, with reference to St. Helen's acts, has especial weight, not merely from his having lived in the same fourth century, but also from the fact that he obtained particular information as to her works in Palestine from his relative Melania the Elder, who had lived there five-and-twenty years.[11]

Quite plain on the subject are the words of the later Nicephorus Calixtus, whose statement, borne out as it is by that of St. Paulinus, has met with general acceptance. Speaking of Nazareth in connection with St. Helen, this writer says: "She came, and *having found the House of the Salutation*, she built there a beautiful church to the Mother of God."[12] Here we must especially take notice that, according to Nicephorus, St. Helen found, not merely the empty site, but the Holy House itself, which he evidently understood to have been enshrined by her within the church she built above it, just as had been done by her and Constantine

---

[10] St. Paulinus of Nola, *Epistola 31 ad Severum.*

[11] M. Chevalier quotes Eusebius, as implying that no other churches had been built in Palestine by St. Helen, except those on Mount Olivet and at Bethlehem. The context makes it clear, however, that in the place referred to (*Life of Constantine*, bk. 3, chap. 43), Eusebius is speaking only of the churches built by her in Jerusalem and its neighborhood. He himself immediately afterward speaks of her progress "round the whole East," everywhere heaping benefits on cities, and so forth.

[12] Nicephorus Callistus, *Ecclesiasticae historiae* (ca. 1320), bk. 8, chap. 30.

with reference to the Holy Sepulcher and the Cave of Bethlehem. She cannot indeed be supposed to have been less careful for the preservation of the house in which our Lord had lived so many years than for that of the other holy places. As to the period before St. Helen's time, no record as to the state of the Holy House apparently has been preserved; although, according to the revelations said to have been made by Our Lady at the time of its removal into Europe, it had been set aside for sacred uses by the Apostles soon after our Lord's Ascension. "This," says Dr. Northcote, "is conformable to everything we know of the habits of the early Christians."[13]

It is true, indeed, as we know from St. Epiphanius, that the Jews, who, after the destruction of Jerusalem, had been driven into Galilee, and particularly those dwelling at Nazareth, bore such hatred to the Christians, that until the time of Constantine they suffered none to live among them. But from this it does not follow, as Canon Chevalier tries to conclude,[14] that in that time of intolerance the Holy House must have been lost sight of, if not actually destroyed. If God desired to preserve it, He surely knew how to defeat the malice of those who would harm it. Moreover, as writes Father Eschbach,

> it scarcely can be doubted that the Blessed Virgin on her final departure from Nazareth left her house to some of her near relatives, and these in turn to their descendants, all of whom would cherish the remembrance of her who was the Mother of Jesus, the founder of the Christians.

[13] Northcote, *Celebrated Sanctuaries*, 73.
[14] Ulysse Chevalier, *Notre-Dame de Lorette: étude historique sur l'authenticité de la Santa Casa* (Paris: A. Picard, 1906), 22.

Hence, considering especially the persistence of family traditions in the East, it is quite natural to suppose that the pilgrims to Nazareth, who from the beginning of the fourth century continued to increase in number, received precise information as to the spot where the Incarnation had taken place.[15]

Even if, as may have been the case, the Holy House was occupied by non-Christians for a time, it would not follow that the traditions regarding it were lost sight of; especially if those that tenanted it were of Our Lady's family.

Like many of the Nazareth houses of the present day, the house of the Holy Family appears to have opened at the back into a cave in the hillside, which thus formed an extension to the house; and in the crypt below the present church of the Annunciation, there is still shown with special veneration this cave or grotto, in front of which the house now at Loreto must originally have stood, the church of St. Helen covering them both.

The church built by St. Helen, though thrown down somewhat later by the Saracens, was still standing when St. Willibald—brother to St. Walburga and afterward bishop of Eichstädt—made his pilgrimage to Palestine about 725. "They came," says his disciple Adalbert, "into Galilee to the village of Nazareth.... There is a church there befitting the sanctity of the place, which has often been bought back by the Christians from the Saracens who would fain demolish it."[16]

---

[15] Alphonse Eschbach, *La vérité sur le fait de Lorette: exposé historique et critique* (Paris: Lethielleux, 1910), 399. To this exhaustive reply to Canon Chevalier we shall have continually to refer.

[16] Chevalier, *Notre-Dame de Lorette*, 30.

We see from the above how soon began the practice of extorting money from the Christians for permission to retain the Holy Places; and this makes it easier for us to understand their continued preservation. For, finding them to be a source of income to themselves, the Saracens were generally wise enough to leave undestroyed the actual shrines, even when they overthrew the churches raised above them.

The date of the destruction of the first church of the Annunciation is apparently unknown; but when Nazareth came into the possession of the Crusaders under Tancred in 1100, there was apparently but little of it standing except the Shrine of the Incarnation in the crypt. Over this the Crusaders built a magnificent basilica, whose foundations, with some portions of the building, still exist. From the accounts preserved to us by pilgrims, we learn that the place of the Annunciation with the actual house in which the Holy Family had dwelt (the House of Joseph, as some of the pilgrims call it) was to be found in this church of the Crusaders in a crypt below the level of the church itself.

The House of the Holy Family had stood, as we have said, immediately in front of the cave now shown at Nazareth; and since the crypt (which, under the Crusaders' church, enclosed both house and cave) must itself have had a cavernous appearance, the steps down to it being cut out of the rock, we need not be surprised to find the place simply spoken of by pilgrims as a grotto, or cave. In this we have the answer to M. Chevalier's objection, drawn from the similarity in this respect of the descriptions of the place given by pilgrims both before and after the date of the translation. To those going there before that event, it was only natural that the place, in which they found the habitation of the Holy Family, should have the appearance of a cave and still more so to those who only saw it after the House itself had gone.

The following more detailed accounts, written by pilgrims of the twelfth and thirteenth centuries, are of value as testifying to the fact of the continued preservation of the Holy House, although their descriptions of the place are not always as clear as we could wish. The first is that of the Russian abbot Daniel, who went to Nazareth around 1107, soon after the building of the Crusaders' church:

> In the middle of the town [the Abbot writes] there rises a large and lofty church with three altars. On entering it you see on the left, in front of a small altar, a small but deep grotto which has two doors, one on the east side, and the other on the west, through which you go down into the grotto. Entering it by the western door you have on your right a cell, the entrance to which is narrow, and in which the Holy Virgin lived with Christ.[17]

The excavations recently carried out at Nazareth have brought to light a portion of the western staircase here mentioned, leading, in the time of Abbot Daniel, to the crypt, or grotto, as he calls it, in which then stood the Holy House. The *cell* here spoken of would seem to be the western portion of the House, which is

---

[17] Quoted by Father Eschbach from *Itineraires Russes en Orient* (Eschbach, *La vérité sur le fait de Lorette*, 415). The plan of the crypt made by Father Vlaminck shows its western stairway "hewn out of the rock" and slanting somewhat to the north. Thus, on descending by it, the pilgrim would find, as Daniel says, the western doorway of the Holy House opposite to him on his right.

believed to have been partitioned off into a separate room for Our Lady.

> In this same grotto [continues Abbot Daniel] near to the western door, is found the place where the Holy Virgin Mary was seated near the door ... when the Archangel Gabriel, sent from God, presented himself before her.... The place occupied by this sacred grotto was the house of Joseph, and it was in this house that everything took place.[18]

Plainer still are the words of Phocas, a monk of Patmos, who visited Nazareth about 1177, and who spent six months within easy reach of it on the neighboring Mount Carmel, where he wrote the following description of the Sanctuary of the Annunciation:

> On the left side (of the church) there is a grotto, which does not go far down into the ground, but is seen near to the surface.... On passing through the entrance to the grotto and descending a few steps, you then have before you the actual house of Joseph, in which the Archangel announced the good tidings to the Virgin. In the place, moreover, in which the Annunciation was made, there is a black stone cross let into white marble, and over it an altar; and on the right side of the altar there is a little room in which the Virgin Mother of God kept herself retired. On the left side of the place of the Annunciation there is seen another room, which has no light, in which our Lord Jesus Christ is said to have dwelt.[19]

---

[18] Ibid.

[19] Chevalier, *Notre-Dame de Lorette*, 36.

Phocas does not tell us whether he went down into the crypt (or grotto, as he also calls it) by its western or its eastern door; but in either case, since there was then no entrance to the cave at the back, except through the Holy House itself,[20] he must have passed at once into this latter; and it is important to observe how perfectly his description of "the house of Joseph" accords with what we are told about the original arrangement of things in the Holy House on its first appearance in the west. Before the time of Pope Clement VII the altar in the Holy House stood, not as now at the east end, but in the middle of its southern wall, and opposite to the now closed doorway, which at Nazareth opened into the cave. Assuming this altar to have been the one spoken of above by Phocas, having on its right the room of Our Lady, this latter must have been formed by partitioning off the part of the house at the west end, in which is the only window. In the same way the part of the House at the other end (originally "at the left side of the same altar"), which has no window, but which is traditionally regarded at Loreto as most sacred, seems to have formed the room "without light" of Our Blessed Lord. Indeed, at Loreto some traces may be still observed of one of the partitions that apparently divided the two end portions into separate

[20] At present a narrow staircase cut in the rock at the back of the cave gives access to it from the sacristy and monastery above. It was made, Quaresimo says, after the Franciscans gained possession in 1620, and was needed to give them safe access to the crypt and its sanctuary; the whole church above being then demolished. The same staircase gives access also to a second small cave, which has since gone by the name of Our Lady's Kitchen, but which cannot really have been connected with the habitation of the Holy Family. This second cave is shown by Father Vlaminck's plan to have lain outside the north wall of the Crusaders' church.

rooms. It seems also, from the earliest descriptions of the Holy House after its translation into Europe, that in it Our Lady's image then occupied a position on the right side of the altar, in the very part, apparently, described by Phocas as the room of Our Lady. At Nazareth, moreover, the recent excavations have led to the discovery, on the spot corresponding to that same portion of the House, of an ornamental mosaic flooring, laid down there, as a Greek inscription states, in the sixth century by a deacon of Jerusalem named Kononos, apparently as an act of special devotion to Our Lady.[21]

Though provokingly brief, the notice of Nazareth about 1120 by another pilgrim, Belardo of Ascoli, is not without its value, as marking the difference there was in structure between the two parts of Our Lady's habitation — namely, between the house itself and the grotto into which it opened. "The cell of Our Lady," says this pilgrim, "into which the Angel entered to her, was a crypt situated at one side of the town; nevertheless, in its interior on the eastern side, it was not constructed of stones, but hollowed out of the rock."[22] Defective though this description is, it at all events implies that, though one part of the habitation was a cave, the rest was built of stones.

As to the fact of the continued preservation of Our Blessed Lady's chamber at the time we speak of, it is confirmed in even plainer words by John, a priest of Würzburg, who wrote his

---

[21] Meisterman, *Nouveau Guide de Terre Sainte*, 375. The flooring of the Holy House, on the translation of the latter, was left at Nazareth.

[22] Eschbach, *La vérité sur le fait de Lorette*, 419. Belardo's words are: "Intus tamen ex parte orientis non ex lapidibus facta, sed sic in saxo cavata." Chevalier is blamed by Eschbach, as disguising the contrast implied by the word *tamen*.

Descriptio Terrae Sanctae, as is remarked by Eschbach, not, after his return to Europe, when his memory of things in the east might have been less exact, but while he was still in Palestine about 1165. After mentioning the opinion held by some, who supposed Our Lady to have been born at Sepphoris, two miles to the north of Nazareth, against them John of Würzburg quotes St. Jerome, as declaring that

> she is said to have been born in the city of Nazareth itself, and, indeed, in the same chamber (*cubiculo*) in which, overshadowed by the Holy Spirit, she afterwards conceived at the Angel's salutation. This chamber [John continues] *is still shown there* in a distinct place, as I myself, when there, have seen and noted.[23]

This passage of John of Würzburg, which occurs in his account not of Nazareth but of Sepphoris apparently has escaped the notice of Canon Chevalier, who, nevertheless, from the preceding paragraph quotes what the same writer says about the mysteries accomplished at Nazareth, although without giving any description of the shrine.

In 1220 the great St. Francis of Assisi is recorded to have made a pilgrimage to Nazareth; and the very terms in which his early biographer records it—"He came to Nazareth to venerate *that*

---

[23] Quoted in ibid., 421, 423. The same writer in a later work has the following: "To the testimonies of these Christian pilgrims must be added that of the Arab traveler Abul Hassan Aly, who, towards the end of the twelfth century, wrote: 'Nassariah is the town in which is to be seen (*oft se trouve*) the *house* of Meriem, daughter of Imran who there was born. This town has given its name to the Christians.'" From Eschbach's *Lorette et l'Ultimatum de M. U. Chevalier* (1915).

sacred House"[24]—testify to the prevalence then of the belief that the actual House of the Holy Family was still there to be found.

Another visit, still more famous, was that paid to it a little later by St. Louis, king of France, who was there for the feast of the Annunciation in 1251, communicating at the altar in the crypt and joining in all the Offices with extreme devotion. The remembrance of this visit of St. Louis has been perpetuated at Loreto by a now faded picture of the holy king painted on the upper portion of the west wall of the Holy House.[25]

Only twelve years after St. Louis's visit to it, the great basilica, which the Crusaders had erected at such cost, was razed by Bibars Bondokhar, sultan of Egypt, who, after overrunning Southern Palestine, invaded Galilee in the spring of 1263, driving the Christians before him into Acre. At Nazareth he caused all those who refused to apostatize to be massacred, and ordered the Church of the Annunciation to be thrown down.

Meantime, however, the Christians continued for another twenty-eight years to hold out at Acre, their last remaining

[24] "Nazaretum pervenit adoraturus Domum illam." Pietro Valerio Martorelli, *Teatro Istorico della Santa Casa Nazarena della B. Vergine Maria e Sua Ammirabile Traslazione in Loreto*, vol. 1 (1732).

[25] After the arrival of the Holy House at Loreto the need of ventilation soon made it necessary to heighten its walls. The fresco of St. Louis, who was only canonized in 1297, is on this added portion. The pictures on it are shown, however, to have been completed before the beginning of the fifteenth century. Eschbach, *Lorette et l'Ultimatum de M. U. Chevalier*, 107. Eschbach thinks it probable that the picture of St. Louis was set up in the Holy House by Charles of Valois, whom Boniface VIII in 1301 made ruler of the March of Ancona. The fresco, he says, bears testimony to the Loreto tradition in the fourteenth century.

stronghold; and the Saracens, unable to dislodge them thence, found it to their interest at times to make truces with them. Thus, in 1282 we find Bibars's successor, the sultan Kelaoun, in his desire to strengthen himself against the Tatar-Mongols, not merely making a ten years' truce with the Christians, but even giving up to them what remained of the church at Nazareth, along with four houses for the reception of the clergy and of pilgrims.[26]

The great church, indeed, had been thrown down to the ground, as Pope Urban IV bitterly lamented in a letter to St. Louis; still it seems from the reports of pilgrims, who took advantage of the truce to visit it, that the actual sanctuary in the crypt had been left much in its old condition, having been, no doubt, protected under God's providence by the solid flooring of the church that covered it.

Among other visitors to Nazareth during this time of truce was a monk of Magdeburg in Saxony, named Burchard of Mount Sion. He was there, apparently in 1283, for the feast of the Annunciation. "There is still remaining," he says in his *Descriptio Terrae Sanctae*,

> at the present day, the place in which the Angel Gabriel brought the salutary news to the Blessed Virgin.... I said several Masses in that place, and on the day itself of the holy Annunciation, when the Word was made flesh. There are three altars in the chapel, and it is of stone hewn out of the rock.[27]

---

[26] F. Laurent, *Peregrinatores Medii Aevi Quatuor*, 4. Eschbach, *La Vérité Sur le Fait de Lorette*, 433.

[27] Est excisa de rupe in petra. Laurent, *Peregrinatores Medii Aevi Quatuor*, 47. These words must not, of course, be understood

Clearer still are the words of the Dominican missionary Ricoldo di Monte Croce, in his account of the pilgrimage made by him during the same truce. "From Acre I came," he says,

> with a number of Christians into Galilee.... Passing through Naim ... we came to Nazareth, and we found a large church almost entirely destroyed, and there was nothing there of the original buildings (*de primis aedificiis*), *except the cell alone* in which Our Lady was announced; that, as a memorial of humility and poverty, *God has specially preserved* (*superreservavit*). There is an altar of Our Lady there in the place where Our Lady was praying when the Angel Gabriel was sent to her, and an altar of the Archangel Michael [sic], where Gabriel stood announcing. After celebrating Masses at both and preaching the word of God, we went and walked through the city.... All these places in Galilee we found from the first to the last in possession of the Saracens (but) peacefully and quietly.... Thence we returned to Acre, the City of the Christians.[28]

The year in which he made this pilgrimage to Nazareth is not mentioned by Ricoldo; but M. Chevalier—whose quotation from him stops short of the words about the "return to Acre, the City of the Christians"—assigns it (without naming

as meaning that the whole chapel was a cave, although the cavernous appearance of the crypt, which seems to have misled some pilgrims, has been already noticed. Burchard is the first to speak of three altars in the crypt. The destruction of the church above it may naturally have led to the erection of additional altars in the crypt.

[28] Laurent, *Peregrinatores Medii Aevi Quatuor*, 105, 107.

any authority) to the year 1294. He thus represents Ricoldo's pilgrimage as made three years *after* the asserted removal of the Holy House; and on the strength of this he quotes him as furnishing "decisive" evidence that whatever there had been at Nazareth before the date of the alleged translation, was still to be seen there three years later. "By a piece of rare good fortune," he writes, "we have a text which mentions it (the Chamber of the Incarnation), which corresponds exactly (1294) with the date of the arrival of the Holy House in the Marches. It is that of Ricoldo di Monte Croce."[29]

If Canon Chevalier had but noticed what Ricoldo says about his return to Acre, he could never have written as above. For, so far from being any longer a "City of the Christians" in 1294, Acre had been so utterly destroyed by the Saracens three years before that date — in May 1291 — that for more than fifty years it remained a simple heap of ruins, while so terrible had been the massacre of Christians that the sea itself had been reddened with their blood. Thus the fall of Acre deprived the Christians of their last footing in the Holy Land.

On the other hand, Ricoldo, who speaks of it as still peacefully in their possession, goes on to tell how, after returning there from Nazareth, he again set out from Acre on a pilgrimage to Jerusalem and other holy places; and, finally, that on his return to Acre from this second pilgrimage, he started thence on a long missionary expedition into Armenia and Persia, the sad news of the fall of Acre reaching him while he was preaching in the far-off city of Baghdad.[30]

---

[29] Ibid., 74.
[30] Ibid., 107–113. Eschbach, *La Vérité Sur le Fait de Lorette*, 447. Ricoldo's *Lament* over the fall of Acre is preserved in the

From all this it is clear that, although the exact date of Ricoldo's pilgrimage to Nazareth cannot be fixed, it was made by him during a time of truce before the siege of Acre, and therefore not after, but *before* the translation of the Holy House, which is assigned to the same May 1291 that saw the Christian city's fall.

What is of especial interest to us in Ricoldo's account of Nazareth is his record of the fact that, of "*the original buildings*"—preserved by the particular providence of God—*there then still remained* the cell in which Our Lady had received the Angel; and this, too, in spite of the demolition of the church above it. A mere cave or grotto could not be called a "building"; and we must therefore take Ricoldo as referring to the little house still standing then in front of the cave, and which he might well indeed describe as "a memorial of humility and poverty."

If it be asked, as it has been by some critics, how can so frail a building as the Holy House be supposed to have withstood the destruction of the church in 1263, it may be answered: (1) that if God desired to preserve it, He certainly knew how to do so; and (2) that, even without any miraculous intervention, it may have been sufficiently protected by the strong flooring of the church above; and the recent excavations made at Nazareth (although still incomplete) seem to give support to this suggestion.

In his report of the excavations, the Franciscan Father Prosper Viaud says: "I have endeavored to prove that this part (viz., the crypt and grotto) was surmounted by a vaulting, which would be able to withstand the downfall of the church, and to protect all that it covered. More than this, I think I have demonstrated

---

Vatican Library, in the form of a letter pathetically addressed to his fellow Dominicans who had there been slaughtered.

that under this vaulting there really did subsist down to this epoch the chamber, or cell, of the Holy Virgin."[31]

Account must be taken also of the avaricious motive that impelled the Saracens to preserve at least something of the sanctuaries, as a pretext for extorting money from the pilgrims to them. "It is evident," further on says Father Viaud, "that in spite of his hatred for the Christian name, Bibars *spared the Sanctuary.* Nor is there anywhere, I believe, an example of the destruction of a single sanctuary by the Musulmans."

We have heard already from St. Willibald's biographer of the sums extorted on this ground from the Christians as early as the seventh century; and the same policy, with reference to the holy places, has more or less ever since been followed by the Turks.

The capture of Acre by the Saracens on May 18, 1291, put an end to any further Christian rule in Palestine, which from that time was at the mercy of the infidels. Eight days, however, before that great catastrophe — for the consolation of the faithful, and to preserve His own former home from further desecration — it pleased God to work the wondrous miracle now to be related.

---

[31] Quoted from Joseph Faurax, *L'abbé J. Faurax, . . . A Lorette, À Lorette!! Le Pape Demande Des Pèlerins. V. Manuscrit de Douai* (1500), *Chapelle de Roccapietra . . . Cheminée de Rouen . . . La Fresque de Iesi . . . Et Autres Documents Inédits,* vol. 4 (1911), 48–49.

Chapter 4

The Holy House Removed
into Illyria (Croatia)

While the Saracens were fiercely pressing on the siege of Acre, and the fall of the doomed city was daily drawing nearer, a very different scene was being enacted among the peaceful hills that border the northeast coast of the Adriatic, in the country known now as Croatia, but in the Middle Ages sometimes as Illyria, sometimes as Dalmatia.

On the morning of May 10, 1291, on the hill on which stands the little town or village of Tersatto, overlooking the seaport of Fiume, the people were astonished to discover a little building where none had been the day before. We feel sure the reader will forgive us for quoting from Father Hutchison the following account of the occurrence, which was abridged by him from the Tersatto historian Pasconi, who, as we shall see, derived his information from contemporary sources.

> The people's surprise [says Father Hutchison] was increased to find that it was apparently a small church, and that its four walls were resting on the earth without any foundation. On the exterior they observed a small campanile on the roof, in which two little bells were hanging.

The walls were constructed of a reddish kind of stone, and were about a cubit in thickness. The building had one door, ten palms high, and six wide.[32] This was on its northern side. On the west was a window, the only one in the house. The house had no pavement or foundations; its roof, which was of wood, was painted of a blue color, adorned with gold stars. Against the walls were some small wooden cupboards, in which earthen vessels and crockery might be kept; and in a cupboard were some vessels of common earthenware, some of which are still venerated at Loreto, and are said to have been used by the Holy Family. Against the south wall was a stone altar, decently arrayed, and with an antipendium of a blue color. Above the altar there was a wooden cross, five palms high, and five wide, at the top of which was fixed the title, *Jesus Nazarenus Rex Judaeorum*. Upon the cross was painted the figure of our Lord crucified. A little below, the *Mater Dolorosa* was depicted on one side of the cross; on the other, the beloved disciple, St. John the Evangelist. Beneath these the Angelic Salutation was written on tablets, one palm wide

---

[32] That is, about 7 feet 3½ inches high and about 4 feet 5 inches wide. The house itself seems to have been originally little higher than this doorway, the walls having been heightened later at Loreto. At Nazareth this cannot have been the *only* door, since there it must have opened, not to the outside, but only into the cave, with which its measurements correspond. But at each end of the Holy House there are seeming indications of other doors built up, apparently answering to the entrances from east and west spoken of by Abbot Daniel. When the truce ended, and Acre was besieged, these doorways may have been built up for safety's sake. One or another of them was apparently still open when Burchard and Ricoldo paid their visits.

and three palms long. At the right hand of the altar was a cedar statue, about two cubits in height, representing the Blessed Virgin, standing with her Son in her arms. Our Lord had the two first fingers of the right hand extended, as if giving benediction; with the left He supported a gold sphere representing the world. A golden crown adorned the heads both of the Mother and the Son, and they were clad in white vestments. In the east wall there was a recess, which, from its bearing signs of smoke, as if of fire, was thought to have served as a fireplace.

Although the people of Tersatto saw that this mysterious building had been brought there miraculously, they must have been still in doubt as to whence it came, or what its original destination was; but Our Blessed Lady herself is said to have removed their doubts by the following revelation.

At that time the incumbent of the parochial church of St. George, at Tersatto, was a certain Alexander de Georgio, or, as he is called in another account, Alexander the Bishop. He was a man of great holiness of life and was very devoted to Our Blessed Lady. Having heard of the wonderful apparition on the hill, he was very anxious to proceed thither; and fearing that his people might be deluded by some deception of the evil one, he prayed that he might be enlightened from Heaven, as to the meaning of all these wonders, while he was unable to gratify his desire of visiting the house, being confined to his bed by a severe malady. He did not pray in vain; for one night the most glorious Virgin appeared to him, surrounded with Angels, and with a benign smile, she thus addressed him: "Be of good courage, my son! Know that the house which has lately been brought to your land is the same in which I was born and brought up. Here, at the Annunciation of the Archangel Gabriel, I conceived the Creator of all things. Here the Word of the Father became man. After my departure from this world, the Apostles consecrated and adorned it, frequently celebrating Mass there. The altar, which was brought with the house, was consecrated by Peter, Prince of the Apostles. The image of the crucifix was placed there by the same Apostles. The cedar statue is an image of myself, made by Luke the Evangelist. This house, which was therefore so dear to God, and which was held in the highest honor for so many years in Galilee, has now come from Nazareth to your shores, by the power of God, to whom nothing is impossible. And now, in order that you may bear testimony to all these things, be healed! Your unexpected and sudden recovery shall be the proof of the truth of what I have been saying."

At these words the Gracious Mother disappeared, leaving behind her a most sweet fragrance.

The vision having disappeared, Alexander was for some time overwhelmed with fear and joy. He then rose from his bed, and found that the malady, from which he had been suffering for years, had entirely disappeared, and that he was restored to perfect health. He hastened to visit the House, and returned thanks for the recovery of his health, telling all that he met of the wonderful things that had happened, and of the inestimable treasure which they had acquired.

About the same time, the Archangel Gabriel is said to have appeared and to have made a similar revelation to a certain holy widow of Tersatto, named Agatha, on whose ground the House was placed.

This wonderful event soon came to the ears of Count Nicholas Frangipani, the Grand Ban of Dalmatia, Croatia, and Slavonia, in whose dominions Tersatto was situated; and he, wishing to be quite certain that the House, which had appeared at Tersatto, was really formerly at Nazareth, determined to send to the latter place and have the site examined. For this purpose he dispatched the aforesaid Alexander, with three companions, to Palestine, that they might ascertain the truth. The four arrived safely at Nazareth, and there they learnt from the inhabitants that the Holy House had gone no one knew whither. They were then shown where it had stood, and the ruins of the great church which St. Helen had built over it. The measurements they found agreed, as did also what they were told about the date of the disappearance of the House from Nazareth. Having thus successfully fulfilled the object of their journey, they returned home, after an interval of four months, and joyfully published all that they had seen and heard; and having again compared the measures they had taken, and the other observations they had made, they unanimously concluded that the House then at Tersatto was the one which had formerly stood at Nazareth.

After this, the same Alexander collected the people of Tersatto in the Holy House, and there, from a pulpit, he related to them the whole history of his journey; and he called God and Our Lady to witness that what he said was not a figment invented by himself, but what he and his companions had seen and heard. His report was enrolled by the orders of Nicholas Frangipani in the chanceries of several neighboring cities.[33]

The joy, however, of the people of Tersatto at possessing such a treasure was to be of but short duration; for on the 10th of December, 1294, after the House had remained there for three years, it suddenly disappeared, and left no sign of whither it had gone. Great was the sorrow of the people at their loss; and in order to console them to some extent, the before-mentioned Nicholas Frangipani erected at his own expense a small church as a model of the Holy House, on the same spot where the House itself had formerly stood.[34]

An occurrence such as that described in the above account could not fail to make a deep, lasting impression on the people among whom it had taken place; and various monuments, erected for the purpose, have perpetuated to the present day the remembrance of it at Tersatto. A chapel more or less of the dimensions of the Holy House, but joined on to a larger church, still marks the site on which it once had rested; and in it above the altar hangs a picture that the following inscription declares to have been sent there by Blessed Pope Urban V, in order to compensate the people of Tersatto for the treasure they had lost:

[33] M. Chevalier (*Notre-Dame de Lorette*, 317) speaks of Count Frangipani as a "problematic personage," insinuating seemingly a doubt as to his reality. The lordly position held by the Frangipani at the time in question and for several succeeding centuries is sufficiently attested by documents quoted by Father Eschbach (*La Vérité Sur le Fait de Lorette*, 249–253). The imposing ruins of their castle are still to be seen outside Tersatto, as well as monuments of members of the family in the Holy Chapel.

[34] Hutchison, *Loreto and Nazareth*, 4–11.

The Holy House Removed into Illyria (Croatia)

"In the year 1367," this inscription says, "the Sovereign Pontiff, Urban V, at the request of the Frangipani, and to soothe the affliction of the Tersatto people, sent through Father Boniface of Naples a picture of the Blessed Virgin painted by the hand of St. Luke upon a cedar tablet."

Another inscription in the same chapel records how, "in the year 1291, Alexander Giorgivich, Incumbent of the parish church of St. George, informed the people of Tersatto and others assembled from the country round of the wonderful translation of the Holy House and of his own miraculous recovery."

On the walls also of the chapel may still be read the following hymn to Our Lady, sung there from time immemorial in the Offices:

> Hue cum Domo advenisti,
> Ut qua pia Mater Christi
> Dispensares gratiam.
>
> Nazarethum tibi ortus,
> Sed Tersactum primes portus,
> Petenti hanc patriam.
>
> Aedem quidem hinc tulisti:
> Attamen hic permansisti,
> Regina clementiae.
>
> Nobis inde gratulamur,
> Digni quod hic habeamur
> Maternae praesentiae.

"The only liturgical hymns written in this meter," remarks Father Eschbach, "are the 'Dies Ira,' the 'Stabat Mater,' and the 'Lauda Sion,' of which all three are of the thirteenth century;

whence it seems lawful," he concludes, "to ascribe to the same period this Tersatto hymn."

It will be more convenient further on to speak of the long-continued practice of the Tersatto people to make pilgrimages to Loreto for the purpose of beseeching Our Lady to *return* to their own place—a practice that would be quite inexplicable, if the Holy House had never been there—but we must not omit here to notice another old inscription bearing testimony to the fact of the translation, which may still be seen on the side wall of a long flight of steps ascending from Fiume to Tersatto. This inscription, which is in Italian, is as follows: "The House of the Blessed Virgin came from Nazareth to Tersatto on the 10th of May, in the year 1291, and left on the 10th of December, 1294." This inscription is attributed, says Father Eschbach, "by some historians to the beginning of the fourteenth century. The common opinion places it in the fifteenth; but it goes without saying that public documents of this kind, so far from originating something new, presuppose, on the contrary, the general acceptance of the facts which they proclaim."[35]

It would be hard to imagine clearer evidence, as to the antiquity and unbroken continuance of the belief of the Tersatto people, than that given by the facts just mentioned.

On returning from one of his visits to Loreto, the present writer happened to meet the late Father John Gerard, S.J., with whom he had some conversation on the subject. The good Father, while owning that he had made no special study of the subject, admitted that his belief in the Loreto tradition had been rather shaken in consequence of the high character borne by

---

[35] See Eschbach, *La Vérité Sur le Fait de Lorette*, 261–265, from which the above inscriptions at Tersatto are here quoted.

some of its impugners. After listening awhile to some arguments in its defense, however, he broke in with the question: "Have you ever been to Tersatto?" and on being answered in the negative: "But I have," he said, and I could not see how to explain what I saw there, if the Holy House had not been really there."

It has been already mentioned that Pasconi, from whom Father Hutchison's account of its brief stay at Tersatto was borrowed, had himself derived his information from contemporary sources. It will naturally interest the reader to know the authority on which this statement rests.

From the year 1453 until the present day, the Sanctuary of Our Lady of Tersatto has continued in the charge of a community of Franciscan Observants, to whom it was originally entrusted by Pope Nicholas V, at the request of Count Martin Frangipani, a member of the noble family already mentioned. Father Pasconi, from whose *Triumphus Coronatae Reginae Tersactensis* Father Hutchison quotes, belonged to this community; and although he wrote as late as 1731, he had abundant opportunities, living as he did upon the spot, both for learning its traditions, and for studying the documents preserved in the convent archives.[36] Unfortunately, the original documents attesting the arrival at Tersatto of the Holy House had then already perished; but Pasconi had

---

[36] Pasconi's work is printed by Martorelli in his *Teatro Istorico della Santa Casa*, as also is Bishop Marotti's *Dissertatio*, in which Glavinich is also quoted. Pasconi is misrepresented by M. Chevalier (*Notre-Dame de Lorette*, 317), as "regretting that no servant of Mary has transmitted to posterity these memorable events," namely, the coming to Tersatto of the Holy House. In reality all that Pasconi regretted was the absence of a record of the *cures* wrought at Tersatto. His history of the Holy House is full of references to Glavinich and other historians of its translation.

happily been preceded by another writer of the same community, to whose work he continually refers, and who had been able to make use of the original documents themselves while these were still in the possession of the convent.

This earlier writer on the history of Tersatto was Father Francis Glavinich, a man of considerable reputation in his day. Born in Istria in 1578, he entered the Franciscan Order at the age of twenty and became guardian of Tersatto Convent in 1607. There he died in the odor of sanctity in 1652, leaving works behind him in Latin, Italian, and Slavonic.

Father Glavinich's *History of Tersatto* was written in Italian and appeared in 1648, although he seems to have been engaged upon it many years before. What chiefly led him to compose it was, he says, the ignorance shown by historians of many things preserved in the Tersatto archives; and he declares that he has bestowed upon it all the care and pains of which he was capable.

The following descriptive title of the book (according to the fashion of the time) reveals its scope and nature: *History of Tersatto containing the true story of the translation of the holy hereditary House of the glorious Virgin from Nazareth to Tersatto, and from Tersatto to Loreto; when, how, wherefore, and by whom it was transported, with some matters more particularly concerning the church and monastery of Tersatto.*[37]

This work of Father Glavinich, in spite of the high standing of its author and its own exceptional importance, is now

---

[37] All that M. Chevalier tells his readers about this book, which he evidently had not seen, is the fact of its publication in 1648. Its title also is given by him incorrectly, as *Historia della Madonna Tersattana*, as if it were merely a history of the picture venerated there.

unfortunately so scarce, says Father Eschbach, "that not even in the great Roman libraries is a copy to be found." Eschbach himself had been unable to set eyes upon it until he got to Glavinich's own Convent of Tersatto. There he was able to peruse it at his leisure, and in the same convent it was seen by Father Hutchison. It seems a matter of regret that these two writers have not given us even longer extracts from a work so rare.

Its special value, as has been said already, lies in the fact that its author had before him the original documents drawn up in attestation of the translation of the Holy House; among them being the report of the priest Alexander on his return from Nazareth, where he had been sent to make enquiries.

"Glavinich affirms," writes Father Hutchison, "that he had seen, read, and made notes of the above Report (of Alexander), which he had faithfully related in his *History of Tersatto*."[38]

The documents relating to the coming and departure of the Holy House, which were still treasured in Glavinich's time, in the Archives of Tersatto Convent, are referred to by him as the *Medoid Papers* (*Memorie Meduidane*), from the fact of their having been for a time removed to an inland fortress named Medoid, when Tersatto, in 1509, had been threatened by the Venetians with bombardment. It was in Glavinich's own lifetime that these precious papers, which had thus been saved from the Venetians and brought back to Tersatto, were accidentally destroyed by fire. Before this, however, Glavinich had already possessed himself fully of their contents, and had taken his notes from them. The account which he gives from them of the coming of the Holy House is thus epitomized by Father Eschbach:

---

[38] Hutchison, *Loreto and Nazareth*, 9.

From the Archives of his Convent, which he calls the *Medoid Papers*, he (Glavinich) relates the unexpected arrival of the Holy House, the revelation made to the parish priest, his cure, the return of Count Nicholas Frangipani, who was then at a distance fighting on the side of the new Emperor (Rudolph I), and his sending the parish priest with three companions to the Holy Land to compare the measurements of the Chapel with those of the foundations left at Nazareth. Pending their return, the Chapel was served by the priest of Fiume and the neighborhood. Four months later the travelers came back into the country, and presented to the Count a report of their expedition and the proofs that the mysterious little edifice really was the former habitation of the Holy Family. Their Report, says Glavinich, is among the *Medoid Papers*.[39]

From this it is clear that, although the papers themselves are no longer in existence, we still have at least the substance of them in Father Glavinich's *History*, and in the works of those who quote him. The story of the unfortunate destruction of the papers is thus told by Father Glavinich himself.

On March the 5th of the year 1629, some drunkard workmen had been brought into our Convent of Tersatto for some necessary work. As a cold north wind, to which our Convent is much exposed, was blowing with great violence, they had been allowed to make themselves a fire, and wine had been served to them. When lo! towards nine o'clock at night, when the religious, being obliged to

[39] Eschbach, *La Vérité Sur le Fait de Lorette*, 273.

rise at midnight for the office of Matins, already were in bed, and whilst the workmen, either from fatigue or from having taken too much liquor, were sunk in a deep sleep, fire broke out in the store-rooms on the ground floor, and, fanned by the wind, quickly destroyed the whole monastery, without its being possible to save anything. Only the sacristy and the church remained untouched.... In this way we lost irrecoverably our annals, the Acts of our Provincial Chapters, the Medoid Documents, and the Report of the journey of Don Alexander, parish priest of Tersatto, who by order of Count Nicholas Frangipani had accompanied the envoys dispatched to the Holy Land. I must add, however, that a few years before this I had taken a certain number of papers from Tersatto, to serve me in my writings, and that these were saved.[40]

The fact that *some* of the Tersatto papers had been saved (as Glavinich here states), explains, apparently, how it was that Pasconi, although writing so much later, was still able to quote from documents preserved in the convent archives. Father Hutchison suggests, moreover, that copies of some of the papers destroyed in 1629 may perhaps have been preserved elsewhere; although Pasconi tells us that the original copies of them, enrolled by Frangipani's order in the chanceries of the neighboring towns of Segna, Modrus, Veglia, Buccari, and Grobnik, had also perished in like disasters either of fire or of war.

A striking testimony to the fidelity with which Pasconi had quoted from authors and manuscripts in the Tersatto archives is

[40] Quoted from Glavinich by Eschbach, *La Vérité Sur le Fait de Lorette*, 275.

supplied by a formal attestation to that effect, signed on February 18, 1735, by the public notary of Fiume city.

M. Chevalier, contending as he does that no such documents were ever in existence, attempts to rob this attestation of its force by referring to it as a simple *acte de complaisance*; and against it he quite irrelevantly cites an answer given to Pasconi on March 25 of the same year by the archivists of the city of Fiume. From these officials, enquiries had been made by Pasconi as to certain papers, extracts from which, obtained "from the Annals of Fiume," are said by the historians of Loreto to have been sent to Pope Leo X. In reply the archivists had declared that "according to tradition their ancient documents had been carried off, no one knew where, by the Venetians when they occupied Fiume."[41]

The term *Annales Fluminenses*, as used by the Loreto writers, included, as we shall see further on, the records both of Fiume city and of the neighboring Tersatto; and Pasconi perhaps had hoped to find in the city archives copies of the Tersatto papers, which, although saved from the Venetians by being taken to Medoid, had perished later in the fire of 1629. In any case, since the answer given by the archivists referred solely to the records of the city, and not to those of Tersatto, it in no way contradicted the testimonial of the notary as to Pasconi's accuracy in quoting the latter.

We may conclude this chapter by quoting from Father Eschbach the highly significant remarks, with reference to Tersatto and the Holy House, made by the learned authors of *Illyricum Sacrum*. In their first volume these writers aptly describe Tersatto as "a town celebrated above all for the stay made there by

---

[41] Chevalier, *Notre-Dame de Lorette*, 424. Martorelli, *Teatro Istorico della Santa Casa*, vol. 3, 31.

the Holy House of Nazareth, which from there was miraculously translated into Picenum."

In their fourth volume they devote three folio columns to the defense of this tradition, from which we need take only the following:

> Apart even from all other arguments, the translation of the Holy House first into Dalmatia, and then into Italy, is placed beyond the reach of doubt by the most ancient, perpetual, constant, and invariable agreement of the two nations; for it would have been impossible for Dalmatians and Italians, who are so widely divided from each other by language, character, and an intervening sea, to agree together both in thought and word and writings with reference to that twofold translation, if it were not true, and too certain to admit of question.[42]

These wise remarks of writers of high standing would seem to us much more deserving of a place in M. Chevalier's work than many of the more or less irrelevant quotations with which he has crowded his pages. Nevertheless, the only allusion made by him to them is the remark that "the authors of *Illyricum Sacrum* had found nothing with reference to it"[43] (namely, to the coming to Tersatto of the Holy House); thus suggesting, says Father Eschbach, to his readers that these grave historians regarded the translation of the Holy House to Tersatto and Loreto, "as a thing that had never taken place," whereas in reality they vigorously maintain its truth.

---

[42] *Illyricum Sacrum*, vol. 1, 143; vol. 4, 94. Quoted by Eschbach, *La Vérité Sur le Fait de Lorette*, 279–280.

[43] Chevalier, *Notre-Dame de Lorette*, 318.

Chapter 5

The Holy House Translated to Loreto

The story of the appearance of the Holy House upon the shores of Italy and of its several changes of position there can best be told in the words of its most famous historian, Father Horace Torsellini, S.J., whose *History of Loreto*,[44] written in elegant Ciceronian Latin, was translated into racy Elizabethan English by Father Thomas Price, a Jesuit upon the English mission. Of this translation of Torsellini's work, published in Paris in 1608, we shall not hesitate to make free use. After spending twenty years at Rome, as professor at the Roman College, under the immediate rule of such superiors as St. Francis Borgia and others of St. Ignatius's own disciples, Torsellini was sent to Loreto in 1584 as rector of the Illyrian College[45] established there by Gregory XIII, and seems to have continued there until his death. He thus had every opportunity of gaining in formation respecting the Holy House,

---

[44] Fr. Horace Torsellini, S.J., *History of Loreto*, vol. 1 (Paris, 1608).

[45] The Illyrian College, which stands at Loreto close to the basilica, was founded for the education, under the shadow of the Holy House, of aspirants to the priesthood of Illyrian or Dalmatian nationality. It is thus of itself a standing witness to the Illyrian tradition as to its temporary existence in their country.

and in his preface he declares that before venturing to write its history he had carefully examined almost every record bearing on it, whether preserved at Loreto, Rome, or Recanati. Of many of the miracles there wrought by Our Lady he was able to speak as an eyewitness. "He is generally called," says Dr. Northcote, "the Father of the history of Loreto, not for his antiquity, but for his painstaking accuracy and completeness."[46]

His *History of the Holy House*,[47] which was published in Rome in 1597, received special praise from Pope Clement VIII and ran through numberless editions, besides being translated into all the chief European languages. Even M. Chevalier admits that the work "has become a classic on the subject, the assertions of which it seemed rash until our own day to call in question."

In spite of this, however, and of his own high personal character, Father Torsellini could not escape the criticisms of Canon Chevalier, by whom all the defenders of the miraculous translation—no matter how high their position in the Church, nor what their repute for sanctity or learning—are set aside, either as dishonest, or as too simple and uncritical to be deserving of attention. Thus, in the case of Torsellini, we find him accused by Chevalier, on quite insufficient grounds, of adding words out of his own head (*de son chef*) to papal bulls and therefore bluntly put on one side as "a witness of no authority."[48] We shall have occasion later on to refer to the bulls in question, which are those of Paul II. "The originals of this Pontiff's Bulls," says Father Eschbach, "have been lost, and they are only known to us

---

[46] Northcote, *Celebrated Sanctuaries*, 90.
[47] Fr. Horace Torsellini, S.J., *History of the Holy House* (Rome, 1597).
[48] Chevalier, *Notre-Dame de Lorette*, 202–206, 369, 490.

from *copies* which differ somewhat in their wording."[49] Thus, the worst that can be said with reference to Father Torsellini is that he may sometimes have been misled by an inaccurate copy of a bull. The injustice of Canon Chevalier's condemnation of him is thus too evident to need remarking on.

The following is Torsellini's account of the arrival of the Holy House in the Italian province of Piceno, borrowed from the quaint English translation of Father Price.

This most sacred House being brought out of Dalmatia into Piceno over the Adriatic Sea, where the passage is near a hundred miles, was seated in a wood of the territory of Recanati, about a mile from the sea, which belonged to a certain matron of Recanati, both rich and godly, whose name was Laureta; of whom ever after being called the House of Loreto, it gave immortal praise to her, from whom it took its name.... [50] In the quiet night the sacred House of the Blessed Virgin was seated in a void place of the aforesaid wood. At which time the shepherds of Recanati, keeping their flocks in the next chase, and dividing the vigil of the night amongst them (as their manner is), suddenly a great light environing the sacred House drew the eyes of the warders to it, to whom it seemed wonderful upon the sudden to see a new house in that solitary place, but especially glittering with great brightness. And there was one among them who avouched that he saw it,

---

[49] Eschbach, *La Vérité Sur le Fait de Lorette*, 302.

[50] Modern writers seem to agree in deriving the name Loreto from *lauretum* (laurel grove). It has been suggested that the lady Laureta spoken of above may herself have been named from the estate of which she was proprietor.

when it came on high over the sea. Wherefore, awaking their fellows to behold the spectacle, first they questioned among themselves (as the fashion of wonderers is), and then with mutual words animating each other to go see what it was, all began to conjecture, as indeed it was, to wit, that it was some heavenly thing. When they came unto it they went into the House itself, and as soon as they had passed the threshold, a great dread came suddenly upon them; but presently, being replenished with a certain unwonted sweetness, they spent the night devoutly in prayer, diligently viewing whatsoever was under the roof.

Whereupon at the break of day certain of them went to Recanati, almost four miles from that place, to relate unto their masters what they had seen. At first for their simplicity they condemned not only them, but also the matter itself, supposing that they related a vain thing. But the shepherds affirming with all asseveration that their own eyes might witness it unto them, if they would, their masters were more willing to believe them and at last went with them to see what it was.

When they came to the place of the wood foretold, and the shepherds' news proved true, none almost believed their own eyes; for in very deed that House was never seen there before, nor newly built, as the antiquity thereof did manifestly show.

With great wonder discoursing thus among themselves, they went nearer to it to behold the roof, to be noted, not so much for fashion, as for antiquity; and greatly admired that such ancient building could stand without a foundation or any support at all. Forthwith putting away these cogitations, they went into the House itself, and suppliantly reverenced the Blessed Virgin embracing the sweet child Jesus in her arms.

Neither did their piety lack her reward. For upon the sudden such sacred dread and joy was poured into them, that they confessed they never felt the power of God more present in all their lives. Whereupon they ran back again to the city with all speed, rejoicing much among themselves that Almighty God had vouchsafed to bestow so rare a gift on them and on their country.[51]

Torsellini then describes at length the eagerness with which the people of Recanati and its neighborhood flocked to visit the sanctuary, so wonderfully placed among them, and the miracles with which their devotion was rewarded: "For by and by the power and virtue of God appeared in curing of diseases, and in restoring of strength to many."

This discovery of the Holy House by the shepherds in the wood took place, the Loreto historians tell us, on the morning of December 10, 1294; and for the eight months following it continued to be there visited by pilgrims; who, without knowing what it was exactly, nor whence it had come, felt, nevertheless, that there was some special sanctity attaching to it; and that great graces were to be obtained within its walls. In the August of the following year, however, it was again moved by the angels, although only to a place in the same district, as we shall see directly.

The place on which it had been first deposited has never been allowed to be forgotten and is still to be seen carefully marked out in a wood near the Loreto railway station. It is still called the

---

[51] Torsellini, *History of Loreto*.

Bandirola, a name that is said to owe its origin to the custom, when the Holy House stood there, of fixing a flag, or banner (*bandirola*), on a neighboring tree to guide pilgrims to it. The exact spot, on which stood the Holy House, is marked by a low surrounding wall of the dimensions of the Holy House, set there to preserve the memory of it by Father Riera in 1575. On another wall, also, at one side, there has been carved a representation of the Holy House borne by angels through the air.

The preservation of this site, with its hallowed memories, throughout so many centuries, is of itself a wonderful confirmation of the tradition as to the miraculous translation of the Holy House; and there still seems to hang about the place a certain atmosphere of sanctity and peace, which strikingly impresses those who approach it with devotion. Loreto writers of the sixteenth century remark upon the multitude of perfumed herbs and flowers that then grew up spontaneously within the enclosure once occupied by the Holy House. The same thing was very noticeable when the place was visited by the present writer in September 1912, both he and his companion being irresistibly impressed by the delicious fragrance that appeared to fill the air—fit symbol of the holiness attached to the place.

We have said that the Holy House was not left very long in the Loreto wood, in which it was first deposited on being brought to Italy. Indeed, only some eight months later it was again lifted by the angels and set down in a field at no very great distance, which lay upon the hill on which Loreto town now stands, and which was then the property of two brothers of a noble Recanati family named Antici.

The circumstances under which, in August 1295, this fresh removal of the Holy House took place are thus told by Torsellini, who thinks that the crimes, which apparently led to it, were especially instigated by the devil in his fury at the increase of devotion occasioned by the coming of the Holy House.

The Chapel of Our Blessed Lady was in a solitary place, near to the sea, and compassed about with a thick wood and high trees. Whereupon certain notorious wretches of desperate boldness, not more allured with the opportunity of preying than stirred with infernal furies, as may be supposed, beset the ways that led unto the sacred House, and began to lie in ambush in places compassed about with thick bushes. From whence rushing forth, they took the pilgrims as they went unto it, set on them unawares, robbed them of their money and clothes, yea, of their lives also, if so be they resisted by force. Whereby in short space all that wood, being infested and notoriously reproached with robberies and murders, was reduced to a wilderness, by reason that the pilgrims were frightened thence; and the reverence and devotion of this holy place growing daily less and less, the most sacred House itself departed thence. For Almighty God, thinking it an indignity that the malice of the infernal enemy should turn to the destruction of mankind the refuge which He had provided for their salvation, He chose a safer and a fitter seat for pilgrims for His own and His Blessed Mother's little House.

There was a little hill, not very steep, almost a mile from that place, nearer to Recanati and not far from the highway, whither the sacred House was carried on high by Angels and placed in the top thereof, about eight months after it was seated in the wood. Two brothers of Recanati possessed the said hill in common with mutual agreement, and taking exceeding joy in the heavenly gift,

The House of the Virgin Mary

began to reverence the most sacred House with brother-like endeavors. And as the mutation of the place and the fame of the new miracle increased admiration, so likewise did it increase the devotion of the inhabitants and strangers. For as soon as it was spread abroad that the House of Loreto had changed [its] place and forsaken the wood, and seated itself on a hill free from thieves and convenient for pilgrims, forthwith it enkindled a desire in the adjoining people to revisit it. Therefore, many flocked unto it from all parts; some had worshipped the same House lately in the wood, and now they reverenced it on the top of the hill, to their great admiration and wonder. For which cause the inhabitants did contendingly reverence this most holy Chapel, venerable as well for ancient wonders as lastly for the miracle of [its] changed seat. And everyone gave Almighty God and His Blessed Mother great thanks that they had not removed elsewhere the most religious House, defiled with robberies and murders; but had set it on a safe hill convenient for the devotion of pilgrims. Whereby the multitude of pilgrims daily increasing, increased also was the celebrity of the sacred House, so that the walls began to be covered with votive tables, with images of wax, with precious hangings, and the altar to be heaped with gifts and money.

But the wealth of the sacred Chapel thus increasing, ... the devotion of those whose fervor should chiefly have increased [lessened]. So that avarice now again made the abode thereof shorter on the hill than it had done in the wood.

The said hill, as we showed before, was common to two brothers, who at first reverenced the most sacred

House godly and devoutly, as was most meet they should. Happy they, if they had used the heavenly gift rather for devotion than abused for gain! For when they saw that the most religious House was adorned with richer donaries, covetousness overcame their greedy minds, and wholly extinguished piety and devotion. Therefore, each supposing that the inheritance of the same hill came wholly to himself, first they began to covet the sacred gold and silver; but afterwards, avarice egging them on, they began to disagree between themselves with more than brotherly hatred. Finally, whilst each strived to get all the commodity for himself, from wrath they fell to arms. And the only thing that prevented the two brothers from defiling themselves and the most majestic Cell of the Mother of God with brother's blood was God's preventing this great wickedness by taking away the occasion thereof.

Wherefore, being no less offended with the discord of these brothers, than with the robberies which were committed in the wood, he removed His Mother's House unto the next hill towards the sea, being about an arrow's flight from that place; and seated it in the very highway that goeth to the haven of Recanati, being also about two miles from the sea. So the cause both of discord and theft was taken away, and at last a steadfast and firm-remaining seat was given to the most sacred House, which stood but a few months in the hill of the two brothers. For it is well known that, within less than a year after it came into Italy, it was seated on that hill where at this present it remaineth.[52]

[52] Ibid.

The House of the Virgin Mary

The site occupied by the Holy House on the hill of the two brothers cannot now be traced as clearly as that of the Bandirola. For the hill of the two brothers "was leveled," says Torsellini, "to fill up the valleys to make them commodious for building, and was also built upon when the town of Loreto was built." Its ancient position is, however, more or less vaguely indicated by a representation of the Holy House placed, at some height from the ground, on the south wall of the papal palace.

Such is the wondrous story of the various translations of the Holy House, as told by Father Torsellini and the other writers to be mentioned presently, and approved by Pontiff after Pontiff.

To anyone inclined to cavil, it is, of course, an easy thing to hold up a story, such as this, to ridicule. Why, such a one may ask, was the Holy House first taken to Tersatto, and then to its other temporary sites, instead of being placed at once where it now is? To ask this, however, is like asking, says Father Hutchison,[53] "Why did not our Lord, in the Gospel, cure the blind man at once? Why did He at first only partially heal him, so that he saw men as if they were trees walking? And it was not until He had laid His hands again upon his eyes, that the blind man saw all things clearly. God works in His own way." "We may observe," remarks Dr. Northcote, in the same connection,

> that supposing the triple miracle to be true, we can see at once what a powerful effect it must have had on the minds of all who were witnesses of it, in the way of predisposing them to believe the extraordinary story, which they were presently to hear, as to what this House or Chamber really was, and whence it originally came. From the first it was

---

[53] Northcote, *Celebrated Sanctuaries*, 56–57.

recognized as a sacred building, belonging in an especial manner to the Holy Virgin, because it contained an image of her, carved in cedar-wood, and an altar, and because of the many favors which were received there by those who called upon her name; but more than a twelvemonth was permitted to elapse before it was made known to them (by means of a vision granted to some pious soul) that it was the very chamber of the Incarnation, which had been once in Nazareth, afterwards transported to Dalmatia, and now brought to Italy. This was a most marvelous history; yet who could say that it was too marvelous to be true, when they had themselves been witnesses of its repeated removal, even within the limits of their own territory, and knew therefore that it was certainly something very sacred, and in a special manner the object of Divine care? Moreover, these repeated translations, if they be true, had the effect of multiplying witnesses of the miracle, or at least evidence of its truth, to an almost indefinite extent. On the whole, therefore, turn the legend which way we will, its texture is such, that what appear at first sight to be its extravagances and extreme improbabilities prove, on a more minute investigation, to be real arguments in its favor; on the theory of its falsehood, they are inexplicable; on the theory of its truth, they receive a rational solution.[54]

We should be hardly doing justice to our subject if we made no mention of the document known as the Letter of the Recanati Priors, about which there has been much disputing; and which, although set aside by the modern attackers of Loreto, seems still

[54] Ibid., 87.

to be looked upon as genuine by others of high authority. If these latter are correct, we have in it conclusive evidence as to the truth of the miraculous translation.

The letter in question, of which Father Eschbach gives a facsimile, is dated September 9, 1295, at which time the Holy House had been for about a month on the hill of the two brothers. It contains the instructions given by the priors or magistrates of Recanati to a certain Master Alexander de Servandis, their "beloved and honored fellow citizen," who was about to set out for Rome; and whom they commission to speak in their name to the Knight Bongiovanni, their agent at Rome, and "with him as soon as possible to go to His Beatitude, and inform him that within these last days the Holy House has been marvelously transported from the wood[55] to the hill of the Illustrious Simeon and Stephan Rinaldi dei Antici." He is to ask the Pope's permission for "the said hill to be made the property of the Community, in order that buildings may be erected on it for the convenience of the devout people who daily come to visit it ... and this the more, inasmuch as there is no peace between the said brothers, as the accompanying attestations show."

We are not told of any action taken by the Pontiff in consequence of this letter; and it may be that, before he had yet come to a decision, the priors had already gained what they desired through the removal of the Holy House from the land of the two brothers on to the high road, where it became, of course, the property, not of any individual, but of the commune.

The letter (which is not mentioned by the earlier writers on Loreto) was accidentally discovered in 1675 at Recanati

---

[55] This shows, if we may trust the letter, that the Pope already knew of its arrival in the wood.

in the archives of the Antici family and was first published by Martorelli,[56] along with an account of its discovery, in 1758. Whatever, therefore, may be thought of it, coming as it did so late upon the scene, it cannot have had anything to do with forming the tradition with reference to the Holy House, since this for centuries before already had been current.

It was found in the secret drawer of an old chest about to be destroyed as useless, in the archives of the noble family to which had belonged the brothers who are mentioned in it, as quarrelling over the possession of the Holy House. The incident was not one to reflect credit on the family; and if it were not true, the letter relating it could hardly have been thought worth preserving by the later members of it, still less worthy of inventing.

With the permission of the present Prince Antici the document was not only examined, but photographed by Father Eschbach. Experts have pronounced the handwriting to be of too late a character for that of the original, declaring it to belong to about 1500. This, however, is no reason for distrusting its fidelity as a copy, the original of which at that time may easily have been in existence. The importance that has been attached to it appears from the fact that another copy of the same, attested by the city secretary, Febo Febi, is found to have been preserved in the public Recanati archives.

In the family archives of the Antici, Father Eschbach found, together with the priors' letter, the written judgment passed upon it on February 7, 1784, by a Roman expert signing himself F.D.M.A., and addressed to an Oratorian of S. Elpidio, Father Fioravanti. The writer of this judgment insists strongly on the importance attached to the letter, which, although a copy and

---

[56] Martorelli, *Teatro Istorico della Santa Casa*, vol. 2, 49–51.

not the original, must be regarded, he says, "as real and genuine," and as of "the same weight as the original itself as an attestation of the facts concerned." While speaking cautiously, Father Eschbach appears to concur in this conclusion; adding from his own examination of the manuscript that "it is written in a free and running hand of the form usual at the time in Italy, with nothing suggesting any attempt to give it a fictitious appearance of antiquity." He observes also that the paper on which it is written shows a watermark, by which a deceit of that sort would have been revealed. All this, he says, proves the writer of it "not to have been a forger." He shows, too, that certain expressions occurring in the letter, which have been represented as not then yet in use, have in reality been found in other papers of the period, while the wording and brusque style of the letter, as well as the titles and surnames occurring in it, are declared by the Roman expert to be such as are found occurring in other Recanati documents of the time. As to the difficulty in supposing Recanati to have had an agent of its own at Rome, Eschbach shows that in the Middle Ages, just as at the present time, it was customary for the business of several dioceses with the Holy See to be entrusted to one common agent.[57]

Until, then, some clearer proof is brought against its authenticity, we seem still to have a right to claim the letter of the Recanati priors among the evidences confirming the Loreto tradition.

[57] Eschbach, *La Vérité Sur le Fait de Lorette*, 325–335; *Lorette et l'Ultimatum de M. U. Chevalier*, 128–133.

Chapter 6

∽

The Historians, the Hermit,
and the Sixteen Envoys

Before continuing our history of the Holy House, a word must first be said in vindication of the character of two of its historians, of whom Canon Chevalier speaks in terms of undeserved disparagement.

The first of these is Jerome Angelita, who, when he died, in 1561, had held the post of secretary and archivist of Recanati city for more than fifty years, having been appointed to that office in 1509. He had, moreover, been preceded in it by his father and his grandfather; and thus, says Dr. Northcote, "he enjoyed many singular advantages for the thorough execution of his task," in writing the history of the Holy House; having "sifted," as he says, "with the most faithful and diligent accuracy all the ancient annals of the Republic."[58] As a standing testimony to the truth of this assertion, "the Recanati Archives contain," says Father Eschbach, "more than fifty volumes of annals in his own handwriting."[59]

The integrity of Angelita's character was admitted even by opponents such as Leopardi, who declared him "quite incapable

---

58 Northcote, *Celebrated Sanctuaries*, 90.
59 Eschbach, *La Vérité Sur le Fait de Lorette*, 43.

of invention"; and testimony to the same effect was borne by no less an authority than the Blessed Peter Canisius, who in arguing against the attacks made on the Holy House by the Reformers, rested confidently on the authority of Angelita, whom he quotes as "one remarkable for his sincerity and for his careful diligence in investigating the facts connected with the history in question."[60]

Angelita's work, entitled *De Almae Domus Lauretanae . . . Mira Translatione*, was presented by him in manuscript to Pope Clement VII on September 19, 1531; and in the dedication of it to the Pontiff he describes it as "a faithful account of the acts of the Empress of the heavenly Court, arranged in order of time and events." The fact of its having been thus presented by its writer to the Pope may surely by itself be taken as sufficiently guaranteeing the sincerity of his narration.[61]

Canon Chevalier, however, whose position is made at once untenable if the reliability of Angelita be admitted, arbitrarily declares that "this historian's recital seems to show nothing that guarantees its truthfulness"; and, as to Blessed Canisius's praise of him, he pronounces it to be "certainly undeserved!" As to the annals of Recanati and Fiume, from which Angelita claims to

---

[60] In his *De Verbi Dei Corruptelis* (1584) Blessed Peter Canisius devotes a chapter, filling eleven and a half folio columns, to the defense of the Loreto tradition.

[61] Girolamo Angelita, *De Almae Domus Lauretanae in Agro Recanatensi Mira Translatione Brevis, and Fidelis Enarratio* (1531). Angelita's work was not published in his lifetime, the first edition having appeared only in 1598. Galeotti's Italian translation of it appeared, however, in 1575, and was the one apparently used by Blessed Peter Canisius. Martorelli gives both Latin and Italian texts in his *Teatro* (1732).

quote, these, says M. Chevalier, have been seen by no one, "and doubtless never have existed." In the same way, as to a certain Schedula, on which Angelita largely rests, and which he says was brought over from Illyria in Pope Leo X's time, it could not, says Chevalier, be found by Vogel, who searched the archives both of Recanati and Loreto; nor is there "any trace of it outside of Angelita's soi-disant history."[62]

In reply to this—with reference to the annals of Recanati, which M. Chevalier says no one has seen—it is enough to remind the reader of the fifty volumes found by Father Eschbach in the Recanati archives written by the hand of Angelita. By the term "Annals of Fiume" (of which town it will be remembered Tersatto was a suburb), Angelita designates the Tersatto papers, of which Father Glavinich's account has been already given. From these had been drawn up, Angelita tells us, the abovementioned Schedula, "brought over," he says, "by certain Illyrians worthy of all credit during the pontificate of Leo X ... containing an account of the first wonderful translation of the Holy Chamber from the city of Nazareth."

This Schedula, he says, "was communicated to His Holiness by letters from the Commune of Recanati"; and of these letters he himself, as city secretary, would naturally be the writer. It was from it, he says, that he took his account of the appearance of the Holy House at Tersatto and of its departure thence; and from the same source, apparently, he gained his information as to the exact dates of these events, which the earlier Loreto writers had not mentioned.

If the Schedula was sent on, as seems to have been the case, to Rome, it is not surprising that Vogel did not find it at Recanati

[62] Chevalier, *Notre-Dame de Lorette*, 314–317.

or Loreto; but in no case could his failure to discover it three centuries later justify the virtual charging of Angelita with invention. Neither does what M. Chevalier says appear to be quite correct, as to there being no trace of the Schedula anywhere outside of Angelita's book; inasmuch as an apparent reference to the incident is to be found in a brief of Pope Leo X, of which M. Chevalier himself supplies us with the text.

It is worthy of remark that, during the first three years of his pontificate, no less than thirteen briefs concerning the sanctuary of Our Lady of Loreto were issued by Leo X; in each of which, however, without any express reference to the Holy House, he bases the granting of his favors on the devotion there shown to Our Lady and the miracles there wrought. After a silence, however, of three years, we find his way of speaking changes; and in a brief of June 1, 1519, in which he renews all the favors granted to Loreto by his predecessors, he seems almost to go out of his way to repeat and emphasize the story of the miraculous translation of the Holy House.

"The most Blessed Virgin," says Pope Leo in this brief,

> having transferred her image and her Chamber by the Divine will from Nazareth, *as has been proved* by the testimony of persons who have a right to be believed; and having placed it first near the Dalmatian town of Fiume, and then in a wood in the territory of Recanati, and then on a hill in the same territory which belonged to private persons; has at last, by stationing it by the hands of Angels on the public road where it now rests, chosen Loreto for herself; and there through her merits does the Most High continually work innumerable miracles.[63]

[63] The Latin text is given by Chevalier, *Notre-Dame de Lorette*, 299.

The incident, told by Angelita, of the coming to Recanati of the Illyrians with their Schedula of extracts from the Tersatto archives, and of the forwarding of the same to the Pontiff, would almost necessarily lead to a reinvestigation of the miracle; and the Pope's words "as has been proved" (*ut comprobatum est*) seem to refer to the fact that such an investigation had recently been held. It must also be remembered that the bringing back of the documents relating to the Holy House from Medoid to Tersatto had taken place about the very time of Leo X's election in 1513. Their restoration to Tersatto would be naturally followed by a fresh examination of them; and this just as naturally by the forwarding of the result to Loreto and to Rome. Enough, at all events, has, I think, been said to show how insufficient are the grounds for charging Angelita with invention.

The other writer, whom we have here to defend against the unfair criticisms of M. Chevalier, is Father Raphael Riera, S.J., whose authority on things connected with Loreto is exceptionally great on account of his long residence there as one of the Penitentiaries, or Confessors.

Riera had joined St. Ignatius, whose fellow countryman he was, in the early days of the Society, and the saint's confidence in him was shown by his employment of him in the foundation of the first Jesuit College at Messina; and again by his selecting him in 1554 to be one of the first Jesuit Penitentiaries at Loreto, where Riera remained until his death in 1582.

His *Historia Almae Domus Lauretanae*, on which he had been engaged for years, and for which he had collected materials from all sides, was still unfinished at his death and was first published by Martorelli in 1732.[64] Great use, however, was made of his

---

[64] In vol. 1 of his *Teatro Istorico*.

manuscript by Torsellini, who often refers to it as *Rierae Annales Lauretani*. For the earlier portion of his history of the translation of the Holy House, Riera had taken great pains to obtain information from Tersatto, having addressed, he says, particular inquiries to the Illyrian clergy in 1564, and "especially to the Prelate holding the chief charge of the place, and to Father Anthony of the Franciscan Convent of Tersatto." From these he seems to have received extracts from the Tersatto papers, which, it must be remembered, were not destroyed till 1629, and to which he refers as the "Annals of the Illyrians." He had been diligent also in questioning the pilgrims, who came to Loreto from Illyria, as to the inscriptions set up at Tersatto to attest the appearance and the disappearance of the Holy House; and it hardly need be said that he took like care at Recanati and Loreto to ascertain exactly the tradition of the place. He was himself, moreover, an eyewitness of some of the miraculous occurrences that he relates; and it was under his direction that the site occupied by the Holy House at the Bandirola was marked out by the low parapet to be seen there still.

M. Chevalier endeavors to weaken the authority attached to Father Riera's work by accusing him of credulity "in accepting every story which makes for the glory of the Holy House." "His criticism," he says, "is non-existent."[65]

Considering the many wonders of which Father Riera was himself a witness at Loreto, it need hardly have been thought surprising if he had been ready to accept somewhat easily what others told him of a similar nature. But if it be meant by M. Chevalier that he made no proper investigation into the facts regarding the miraculous translation, we have seen that this is

---

[65] Chevalier, *Notre-Dame de Lorette*, 353.

contrary to the truth. With perhaps more reason, M. Chevalier complains of the "vagueness" of Riera's references to authorities; and it is true indeed that, not having modern critics in his mind, he does not sometimes give the text of documents we should have liked to have, and states less precisely than would now be expected where they were to be found. In the case, however, of one such as he, whose whole character excludes the supposition of deceit, this is surely no sufficient ground for refusing, as does M. Chevalier, to accept his testimony even upon matters that came directly under his own observation.

Having said this much in defense of these two writers, whose authority till recently was universally admitted, we may now continue our narrative, leaving other unjust criticisms of M. Chevalier's to be dealt with as we proceed.

The final removal of the Holy House to the spot where it has ever since remained took place, we saw, before the end of 1295. While seeing, of course, that it was a chapel dedicated to Our Blessed Lady, the people on whose land it had been so wonderfully placed were necessarily ignorant for a time as to its real nature and history. They seem to have received their first enlightenment from some of the good Tersatto people, who had never ceased to bewail its disappearance. The story is thus told in Father Price's translation of Torsellini:

> News of the House of Loreto and of her wonders being reported in Sclavonia by certain merchants, enkindled the Dalmatians to visit the House that was so glorified with miracles. Whereupon certain of them, beholding the Chapel of Loreto, acknowledged it, not unwillingly, to be the same; and sighing with the desire they had to see their lost treasure, thus began to bewail their late loss:

The House of the Virgin Mary

"This House, which is now honored in Piceno, was lately reverenced in Dalmatia. This native House of the Blessed Virgin was first carried by heavenly power from Galilee into Sclavonia, that afterward the Picentians might have it brought unto them. This wonder was showed to the Dalmatians by a heavenly sign, and made manifest by certain men sent into Galilee."

But because these and suchlike speeches of the Sclavonians were strange and wonderful to the Picentians — for as yet they had heard nothing of her transmigration from Nazareth and Dalmatia — many esteemed them vain and foolish. But in a short time a new wonder from heaven declared them to be true indeed.

Near to the wood and seat, which the Blessed Virgin Mother of God did first make choice of in Piceno, there is a little hill called Mont Orso, whither a holy man of great sanctity had retired himself; who, being wholly devoted to Our Blessed Lady, came daily to visit her seat of Loreto, where he spent many hours in devout prayer. He gave diligent care to those wonderful things which the Dalmatians had published with great asseveration. Now and then also he heard the Dalmatians themselves lament their mischance, and bewail the loss of their nation, that the native House of the Blessed Virgin was taken from them. The godly Hermit was amazed when he understood that it was her native House. And truly the thing to him seemed almost incredible, but yet worthy to be enquired of with all diligence. And having a vehement affection to know the truth, and to increase devotion to Our Blessed Lady, he desired to understand from heaven whether that were true or false. Whereupon without delay he punished his body with fasting, with haircloth and stripes, gave himself to prayer, and omitted nothing whereby he thought he might please and pacify Almighty God; specially he prayed and besought the Blessed Virgin Mother of God by some certain sign to manifest what Chapel it was, or from whence it came.

Neither did the Blessed Virgin frustrate his inflamed piety and desire. For the second year after the coming of the sacred House into Italy, Our Blessed Lady appearing unto him in his sleep, and bidding him be of good comfort, told him that in Italy she had chosen a seat for the little House, wherein she herself did live on earth; which, because it was negligently reverenced in Galilee, was now by the ordination of Almighty God transported thence by handwork of Angels, that it might be brought into Dalmatia, and so into Piceno itself. There she herself was born, and there also did she conceive the Divine issue; for which cause that House was and ever shall be dear to God and herself. She likewise declared all that she had related to Alexander, Bishop of Tersatto,[66] in his sleep, as before hath been said; concluding at last that by the special grace and favor of the Almighty that heavenly gift was given to the Picentians and Italians, as a solace to their evils, and as a most certain refuge and defense unto all nations in the perils of this mortal life; commanding him to go and to declare these things to the citizens of Recanati and to the adjoining people.

---

[66] In the original *Tersactensi Antistiti*. Alexander's precise ecclesiastical rank is uncertain. Angelita and Riera also describe him as *Sacrorum Antistes*, which does not necessarily mean a bishop.

The House of the Virgin Mary

Wherewith awaking out of his sleep with exceeding joy of mind, he straight fulfilled the commandment of the Blessed Virgin. And first going to Recanati, he declared his vision to the people of the city, protesting that Our Blessed Lady herself was the author of his speeches. Leaving the people of Recanati in a wonderful maze, he made great haste unto other places to declare the same to them. But at first the Picentians esteemed it a vain fancy, and many reputed the reporter for a teller of vain dreams. Yet afterwards because about that time there was a rumor that this very Chapel was given and taken again from the Dalmatians by the handwork of God, and also how the Dalmatians themselves acknowledged it at Loreto, they remembered themselves, and thought that so weighty a matter was in nowise to be neglected. And likewise calling to mind the late wonder, how the most sacred House had changed her seat three times in one year in their own territory, they were moved therewith to send messengers to and fro to enquire thereof. And at last, the citizens of Recanati propounding the matter, it was decreed by common advice of the Picentians that, with general contributions of money, certain men should be sent into Sclavonia, and from thence to Galilee, to seek out the truth of the matter by the testimony of their own eyes and other certain and manifest tokens.

Sixteen men, honorable for faith, religion, and authority, were chosen out of all Piceno; to whom commandment was given that, first enquiring in Dalmatia, and then in Galilee, they should diligently seek out the whole matter, and should bring them word of all that they found concerning the native House of the Blessed

Virgin, which was said to be in those parts. Who, forthwith passing the Adriatic Sea and arriving at Tersatto, opened to the inhabitants the cause of their coming, who yet smarted with the grief of their late wound, and lamented to remember that such a treasure was taken from them. At the entreaty of these ambassadors they showed them the floor, and the house which they had built very proportional and like to that of Loreto for a monument thereof. Whereupon the Picentian ambassadors applying a measure of the House of Loreto, which for that purpose they had brought with them, to every side of the vacant space, found it in all respects agreeable to the House of Loreto. Then demanding of them how long since the most sacred Chapel departed from them, they assuredly knew that, at the very same time that it was taken from the Sclavonians, it was given to the Picentians.

So out of hand the ambassadors, returning again to sea, and sailing along by Corcyra, Crete, and Cyprus, arrived at Palestine with good success. And understanding that the ways were nothing secure by reason that the Turkish armies wandered up and down all Syria, they hired a convoy which conducted them safe into Galilee, and from thence back again to their ship. Coming to Nazareth they enquired of the native House of Our Blessed Lady, and diligently demanded of it of the Christians, who, such as they were, dwelt in the midst of that depraved nation; who brought them to the desired place, that they might behold the floor, with the foundations of a house raised up from thence, yet in the ground to be seen; which, measuring with very diligent care, they found that in every respect all things did agree with the impressions left in Sclavonia, with the floor and the walls of the House of Loreto. And having dispatched their business in both places, they shipped themselves with great gladness, and with happy passage were carried safe to Ancona, whence they set forth.

Whereupon making haste home, and relating all that they had found to the Magistrates and Governors of the cities from whence they were sent, they imparted unto them what great joy they conceived therewith. And the citizens of Recanati, desiring to have a monument there to remain, registered the whole matter in public record, adding thereunto the names and testimonies of the sixteen ambassadors, that the matter might be well witnessed to all posterity. Certain copies whereof being reserved in the houses of private men are yet to be seen. And thus much was known and found by these ambassadors the year of our Redemption, 1296.[67]

As to the measures taken by the Magistrates of Recanati to secure the remembrance of the wonderful occurrence, the following additional details are recorded by Riera, who, after relating the return of the sixteen envoys, says:

The Recanatensians, in order to perpetuate the memory of so great an event, drew up a public *Diploma*, or *Instrument* (*Instrumentum*), as they call it, in which the whole thing was told in order: How, viz., in order to establish the truth regarding the sacred Chapel, they had dispatched into Illyria and Asia sixteen envoys, whose names were there

---

[67] Torsellini, *History of Loreto*, vol. 1, chaps. 11–13.

given; what these had done; when they had returned; and on what evidence they had proved the truth of each thing told above. A public Decree was also issued by the Magistrates, requiring each of the chief citizens to preserve in his own house an official copy of the *Instrument*, accurately written upon parchment. Of these, some copies have been preserved at Recanati down to our time. For in addition to many others, who give full testimony to the fact, the most excellent Doctor Bernardino Leopardi, one of the noblest citizens of Recanati, has assured me, in this year of our salvation, 1565, that he has often seen and read the copy which his grandfather, or at any rate his ancestor, had then received, transcribed by the Secretary of the Commune.

If (as Canon Chevalier would have it thought) no such documents had ever been, how can it be supposed that Riera would have thus appealed to the knowledge of them, not only on the part of the Dr. Leopardi, whom he names, but of many others also still living at Recanati when he wrote in 1565? M. Chevalier, however, being unable to meet this direct testimony in any other way, has actually the assurance to accuse this much respected Jesuit historian of having *invented* these details![68]

We may indeed regret that, not foreseeing the requirements of modern criticism, Father Riera did not think it necessary to present us with the text of the document in question, instead of merely assuring us of its existence; but with reference to a matter, which thus fell within his own personal knowledge, his

---

[68] Chevalier, *Notre-Dame de Lorette*, 320 note. "Riera le Premier a inventé ces details."

word cannot be called in question; and it is surely an unpardon-able thing on the part of Canon Chevalier to accuse him of invention. In the next chapter we shall see how it came about that the original *Instrumentum* in the archives of the city was unhappily destroyed.[69]

[69] Father Cesare Renzoli, S.J., who in 1697 wrote *Santa Casa Illustrata e Difesa*, says that he learned from a member of the Leopardi family that *their* copy of the *Instrumentum* had been lost by lending it to a relative. He therefore expresses the hope that it may yet be in existence (Martorelli, *Teatro Istorico della Santa Casa*, vol. 2, 351). We have made no mention of a paper found at Recanati in 1674, but quite unknown until that time, which professed to be a letter, written in 1297 by the hermit who received the revelation spoken of above, and containing an account of the arrival of the Holy House and of its several changes of position. The whole style of the letter, says Father Eschbach, shows it to be not earlier than the middle of the fif-teenth century. He agrees, however, with the Abbot Trombelli in remarking that, if it was a forgery, it proves at all events how general, at the time of its concoction, was the belief in the miraculous translation; no protest having been made against it. Eschbach, *Lorette et l'Ultimatum de M. U. Chevalier*, 127.

Chapter 7

The First Additions to the Holy House
and the Ghibelline Violators

As the fame of the miracles connected with the Holy House, and of the sacred character attached to it, became more widely spread, so naturally did the number of the pilgrims flocking to it grow, as also the need of making provision for their shelter. The first anxiety, however, of the Recanati authorities—when they began to realize the treasure that Our Lady had committed to their care by placing it on *their* high road—was to secure the safety of the little building, which, without foundations of its own, rested simply on the ground. For this purpose, to save it from the danger of falling in, they surrounded it with a strong wall of brick resting on firm foundations. This, Angelita tells us, was done without even waiting for the return of the sixteen envoys, and therefore not later than the year 1296. In connection with the building of this wall made of bricks, it may be noticed that the only building in Loreto made of stone is the Holy House itself. All the rest—including the basilica and the papal palace, and even the upper layers, which after its arrival at Loreto were added to the walls of the Holy House itself—are made of bricks. The significance of this fact is too evident to demand remark.

The House of the Virgin Mary

When the surrounding wall was finished, it was found, says Riera, to the amazement of the people, that it had separated itself from the Holy House far enough to enable a boy to pass all the way round between it and the House. This fact was fully certified two centuries later when the wall came to be taken down; as Riera was himself assured by the architect Nerucci, who had had to execute the work.[70]

Upon this protecting wall, Riera tells us, frescoes were painted by the Recanati people representing the whole history of the translation, in order thus to perpetuate the remembrance of the miracle; and these frescoes were still in existence when Angelita wrote his history and are mentioned by him among the sources from which he derived his information. There they remained until the wall itself was taken down in 1531, in order to give place to the marble casing enclosing the Holy House at present. The pictures on the north surrounding wall seem, from what Riera says, to have been then still in fair preservation, although those on the other sides had been much blackened by smoke from the votive candles.

Covered porticoes were next erected around the wall just mentioned, both to provide some shelter for the pilgrims and to make room for their votive offerings; and beneath the portico upon the southern side a second altar was erected at which Mass could be heard by the crowds who were obliged to kneel outside.

There was still but the one doorway into the Holy House, in the middle of its northern wall, and immediately opposite to the altar consecrated by St. Peter. Over this latter hung the curious square cross with the painting of our Lord upon it, now placed on the west wall above the little window; and seemingly on the

---

[70] Martorelli, *Teatro Istorico della Santa Casa*, vol. 1, 34.

right side of the altar, as it had been at Tersatto, was the niche containing the image of Our Lady.[71]

Except, therefore, for the abovementioned encircling wall and porticoes, the Holy House had not as yet apparently been enclosed within any larger church, when in the year 1313 the troubles now to be related came upon Recanati.

Italy at that time was harassed by the war between the Ghibellines and the Guelfs; the former sided with the emperor in his encroachments on the Holy See, and the latter supported the cause of the Pope and the Church. Recanati had so far shown itself loyal for the most part to its lawful sovereign, the Pope; but the Ghibelline party in the city unfortunately gained the upper hand in 1313 and contrived to hold it for some years, during which time atrocious crimes were committed. Not only did the faction then dominant refuse obedience to the governor of Piceno appointed by the Pope, but when the bishop of Recanati urged upon his flock the duty of submission, he himself was driven from the city and his palace was sacked. In fact, so virulent a spirit of irreligion took possession of the Ghibelline party then in power as to lead them deliberately to select the feasts of Our Lady for raids upon the Holy House itself, which is spoken of in the document we are about to quote as "the church of St. Mary of Loreto."

The document in question consists of the judgment that was passed two years later upon the Ghibelline leaders by the Pope's representative, at the neighboring town of Macerata, and which was copied by Vogel from the manuscript itself, dated October

---

[71] See ibid., vol. 1, 135, 49, 517; vol. 2, 13, 32, 33. The altar was only moved to the east end by Clement VII, by whom also the present doors were opened and the ancient one built up.

23, 1315. That the church mentioned in it as Sanctae Mariae de Laureto, and described as "belonging immediately to the Church of Recanati and the *mensa* of its Bishop," can have been none other than the little edifice known to us as the Santa Casa is fully admitted by Canon Chevalier and his fellow critics.[72]

In the papal judge's sentence, the leaders of the Recanati Ghibellines are declared, among many other crimes committed during the two preceding years, to have invaded the abovementioned church on all the feasts of Our Blessed Lady and their octaves, at the head of armed troops on horse and foot; and of having carried off the money placed in the collecting box, and the votive offerings left by pilgrims on the altar and on the images of our Lord and Our Lady.

This judgment on the crimes of the Ghibellines was found by Vogel in the secret archives of the Recanati Senate, having been removed there apparently at some later date from Macerata. The full text of it occupies nine pages in his work *De Ecclesiis Recanatensi et Lauretana*.[73]

Its publication did not put any immediate stop to the disorders, and in the disturbances that followed a number of the faithful citizens were expelled or massacred. In 1319 the Marshal of the Marches, when sent by the papal governor to treat with the rebels, was treacherously murdered, and his death was followed at Recanati by the massacre of more than three hundred of the Pope's adherents, some of whom, after being dragged through the streets by the feet, were buried alive on the site of their own demolished houses. To reestablish order, troops had to be sent

---

[72] Chevalier, *Notre-Dame de Lorette*, 156.
[73] Vol. 2, 68–77, and vol. 1, 306; published in 1859, forty years after Vogel's death.

against the rebels, and in 1322, the troops burned Recanati to the ground.[74] It was in this unhappy conflagration that the city archives containing the report of the sixteen envoys, and other papers relating to the Holy House, were destroyed; although some copies, as we have seen, were happily preserved.

To return, however, to the Macerata judgment of 1315. With reference to the Holy House, the document is of great value, not merely as testifying to the celebrity already attached to the sanctuary within twenty years of its arrival on the shores of Italy; but even more, if I am not much mistaken, on account of there occurring in it a singular expression, which seems not yet to have attracted the notice it deserves. The document is written in the medieval Latin of the period, although, in describing the articles stolen by the marauders from the shrine, such half-Italian words are used, as *guillandras* for wreaths or garlands, *bindas* for bands, *syrico* for silk, and so forth.[75]

These votive offerings are mentioned as consisting of candles and torches, images of wax and silver, wreaths also of silver — some of them adorned with pearls — and of silken bands and veils and cloths; and they seem to have been so numerous as to cover the walls of the porticoes or cloisters, which had been put up around the Holy House. Each time the marauders paid their sacrilegious visits, moreover, they found apparently fresh offerings to carry off; which shows how assiduous and undaunted were the pilgrims in paying their devotions there.

---

[74] For a full account of these events see Eschbach, *Lorette et l'Ultimatum de M. U. Chevalier*, 170–194. The crimes of the Recanati Ghibellines are enumerated in Pope John XXII's Constitution of August 25, 1319.

[75] In Italian, *ghirlanda, benda, serico.*

But what seems especially deserving of attention is an unusual term used by the judge, who speaks of the marauders as having snatched the ornaments upon the image of the Blessed Virgin, *and from her Cona* (*et de Cona ejus*); and "upon the image of our Lord Jesus Christ, which was *in the said Cona*" (*quae erat in dicta Cona*).

How are we to understand this curious word *Cona*, here twice occurring and used apparently with emphasis?

The various meanings of the word given by Du Cange will none of them make sense here;[76] nor do we find more satisfactory Vogel's suggested explanation, who puts opposite to it in the margin "*in dicta statua.*" For—to say nothing of the incongruity involved in speaking of one statue as if it were in another—*Cona*, at all events as used in the first of the two instances, plainly does not mean statue; since it there evidently points to something distinct from Our Lady's image.

It seems also clear that, in whatever sense the word be taken, it is here used as indicating something not merely distinct from the two images, but something *within which* they were each of them contained; for our Lord's image is distinctly stated to have been *in* the Cona of Our Lady.

As to the image of our Lord here mentioned, everyone who is familiar with the Holy House and the sacred objects it contains, will, I am sure, understand the image spoken of to be the large, square Cross with the figure of Him painted on it,[77] which has

---

[76] The meanings given by Du Cange for *Cona* are "pitchfork," "sheaf," "a liquid measure," "climate," "figure," and so forth.

[77] It may perhaps be useful to remind the reader that the Latin word *imago*, like the Italian *immagine*, is used indifferently for "picture" or "statue."

always been an object of special veneration in the Holy House, and which, according to the revelations said to have been made by Our Lady both at Tersatto and Loreto, had been there placed by the Apostles.

For the last four centuries these two images of our Lord and Our Lady have faced each other at the two ends of the Holy House, where they were placed by Pope Clement VII; and a glance at the picture of the cross (which measures some three feet eight inches each way), will make sufficiently apparent the impossibility of supposing the two images to have been ever set in one same niche or reredos; although this has been suggested as the meaning here of *Cona*, by some evidently unacquainted with the actual things in question. In fact, in the earliest descriptions of them, both at Tersatto and Loreto, the two images are spoken of as each occupying its own separate position, the cross fixed above the altar and Our Lady's image in a niche on the right side.

It is necessary, therefore, to look elsewhere for an explanation of the word *Cona* in the Macerata sentence, where it is clearly used with no indefinite significance, but as marking something that was an aggravation of the crime.

Now, as everyone acquainted with Italian knows, in a host of words the Latin *u* has come in Italian to be softened into *o* — as, for example, in *secondo* for *secundus*; and even in ancient documents in Latin nothing is more common, says Du Cange, than to find *o* used for *u*, of which he gives as examples *jobemur* for *jubemur*, *docalis* for *ducalis*, and so forth. And in the very document we are concerned with we find *derobando* for *derubando*, just as *bindas* has in the same to stand for *bendas*, *syrico* for *serico*, and *ymaginem* for *imaginem*. If, then, we take *cona* in the same way to be meant for *cuna*, the word becomes at once, not merely significant, but particularly applicable to the case in question.

For the Latin word *cuna*, "cradle" (in the classics usually plural), is used in Italian to mean birthplace, abode, or home; and is so used by Dante, who flourished at the very time of the giving of this judgment.[78]

In a document, therefore, that contains, as this does, many half-Italian words, *cuna* may well be taken to be used in its Italian sense. We have seen that the Holy House, both at Tersatto and Loreto, had been proclaimed to be Our Lady's *birthplace*, her *natalis Domus*, or *native home*, as Torsellini continually calls it. What, then, could be more natural than that the judge should lay stress upon the fact that the outrages had been committed in the very *birthplace*, or *home*, of Our Blessed Lady? But, if this be the case, this document supplies us with contemporary evidence of the fact that, even in the first years of the fourteenth century, the Santa Casa was already well known to have been the dwelling place of Our Lady, although M. Chevalier would have us think that such an idea was never thought of for more than a century later. The suggestion made above as to the meaning of the word in question is put forward here conjecturally, in the hope that it may stimulate enquiries.

At the same time, I can but confess my inability to see how else to understand it, if any real meaning is to be given to it.

As to the veneration paid to the wooden cross found in the Holy House on its translation into Europe, Riera, writing about 1570, tells the following:

There is still living in the town of Castel Fidardo a man named Giovanni Tomaso, venerable for his age and

---

[78] "Inferno," canto 14, line 100. See also Dellacrusca, *Vocabulario*, art. "Cuna."

gravity of character, who in his younger days being accustomed frequently to visit the Holy House of Loreto, heard that the following miracle had taken place with reference to this image of the Crucifix. Some of the officials attached to the Holy House had felt dissatisfied at the old and worn appearance of this most holy Cross, the majesty of which was in many ways obscured; and for this reason they had ventured to remove it from the sacred Chapel into a more conspicuous place in the great church. But by the act of God it went back on the following night to its old position. The officials, however, thinking this due to some mere human agency, removed it once more from the sacred Chapel to the same place; but by an evident miracle of God they understood that it had been restored to its own place by the holy Angels.[79]

The amount of credence to be given to a story such as this depends, of course, upon the greater or lesser value of the authority on which it rests. Nevertheless, it shows in any case the unusual veneration with which this image of the crucifix has been regarded from the first.

It was placed in its present position, above the window of the Holy House, at the time of the alterations made by Clement VII. There it is above the reach of those who pay devotion to it. In its old position, however, above the original small altar, it had been within their reach; and Riera says that the painted figure of our Lord had been almost effaced, from the feet up to the knees, by the kisses of the pilgrims.

[79] Martorelli, *Teatro Istorico della Santa Casa*, vol. 1, 145.

Chapter 8

∞

The First Church Built
over the Holy House

The terrible chastisement that had been inflicted on the people of Recanati by the destruction of their city put an end to their revolt against the Pontiff; and after receiving from them a deputation expressing their repentance, Pope John XXII granted permission, in 1328, for the rebuilding of the city, although at first without fortifications. The excellent laws, passed in that same year by the Recanati Senate for the repression of crime and for the promotion of religion, are quoted by Vogel; and at length in a bull full of praise for the repentant people, Pope Innocent VI, in 1356, restored the bishopric, which had been removed during the interval to Macerata.

The Holy House, situated as it is about three miles from Recanati, seems to have been preserved from any more substantial injuries than those mentioned in the last chapter; and after the defeat of the Ghibelline party the citizens appear to have set no bounds to their devotion to it. Great numbers of them, says Angelita, in spite of the distance, insisted on paying a daily visit to it, while the little children were taught each morning on rising from their cradles to salute Our Lady of Loreto as their

Mother. For the benefit also of the old and feeble, who had not strength to make the journey to Loreto often, an altar was put up in St. Gabriel's Church at Recanati, with a picture over it of Our Lady of Loreto; and an indulgence was obtained from Pope Benedict XII, in 1341, for all those who visited it. The document bestowing this indulgence, "written in letters of gold, and almost consumed by decay and age, I myself," says Angelita, "found in the Recanati Archives."[80] From this we see that, even during their residence at Avignon, the Popes were not unacquainted with what had happened at Loreto.

At this same period, also, we learn from Riera that the bishop of Macerata, who then included Recanati in his diocese, caused a little book in simple style to be composed, containing an account of the appearance of the Holy House and the other events connected with it, which teachers were instructed to use in their schools, in order thus to train the children to look upon Our Lady of Loreto as their Mother from the first. Although now lost apparently, this book was still extant in Riera's time, "very ancient copies of it," he says, "having been found in our days

---

[80] Here again, with systematic injustice to the Loreto writers, we find M. Chevalier declining to take Angelita's word, even with reference to a document found, as the latter says, by himself in the archives of which he was the custodian. He alleges (1) that in such matters letters of gold are unknown to pontifical diplomacy; and (2) that the bullarium of Benedict XII, at the Vatican, shows no trace of such a document. Father Eschbach's reply to this is that Angelita does not call the document in question a bull or an apostolic letter; and he shows from his way of speaking of it that the Pope, in granting the favor, had most likely only put his name to the petition presented to him by the Recanati envoys. Martorelli, *Teatro Istorico della Santa Casa*, vol. 1, 525; Eschbach, *La Vérité Sur le Fait de Lorette*, 191.

at Recanati."[81] Its author, according to Martorelli, was Blessed Peter, a Franciscan, bishop of Macerata from 1328 to 1347, who when the Holy House arrived in 1294, must already have been of middle age, since at his death, in 1347, he had reached, Ughelli says, his ninetieth year.

As further proof of the quickness with which the pilgrimage to Loreto became famous, and as showing, at the same time, how well the true nature of its sanctuary was soon understood, Father Eschbach quotes a will made on August 22, 1348, by Peter Guido Roggeri of the little town of Jesi, near Ancona, bequeathing money in order "to help pilgrims to the Holy House of Mary to pay the tribute exacted from them for passing through the country."[82] There can be no doubt, says Father Eschbach, as to the sanctuary indicated in these terms; and we see from this that, in the first half even of the fourteenth century, the little church was already known by its distinctive appellation of the *Holy House.* M. Chevalier is therefore clearly wrong in placing the first appearance of the word *domus* in connection with the Loreto Church ninety years later, in a document of 1438 recording the penance imposed on a blasphemer by the vicar-general of Osimo, "ut Domum sacratissimam Mariae de Laureto corporaliter visitaret."[83]

---

[81] Riera, *History of Loreto*, chap. 7. What Martorelli has given as Bishop Peter's account of the Holy House, is really, as Father Eschbach shows, a little treatise for the use of pilgrims by a Spanish Jesuit, Father Loarte, published in 1575. Martorelli was misled by a copy of Loarte's treatise, found among a collection of old papers with a wrong heading prefixed to it. *La Vérité Sur le Fait de Lorette*, 342–344.

[82] Ibid., 198–202.

[83] The term *almae domus* in the plural was sometimes applied to the houses for the clergy and the sick erected around the

In connection with the abovementioned will of the good citizen of Jesi, who in 1348 left money to assist the pilgrims to Loreto, we must not fail to notice the fresco representing the translation of the Holy House, which has been recently discovered on the wall of the abandoned church of St. Mark outside the walls of the same ancient town of Jesi; and which competent authorities pronounce to have been the work of a painter of Giotto's school of that selfsame period. Professor Cesare Annibaldi is quoted by Father Eschbach as declaring: "The fresco of the church of St. Mark most certainly represents the translation of the Holy House of Loreto. Without any doubt it dates from the first half of the fourteenth century."[84]

The need of a larger church for the reception of the pilgrims, so constructed as to contain within it the Holy House as the central object of devotion, must have been very early felt; and the building of the first church so erected—spoken of from its oblong figure as the *Ecclesia Oblonga*—appears to have been commenced about 1350, or very shortly after. In a will dated December 28, 1355, there is mention of a legacy to the church "*Sanctae Marie de Laureto in ipsis aedificiis*"; which seems to show that it was then in course of actual erection. Another legacy in 1383, toward the purchase of a bell, appears to mark the period of the completion of this oblong church, which stood until the

---

church. On the strength of this, M. Chevalier, without bringing any proof to support it, proceeds to the conjecture that from these houses the name became gradually given to the sanctuary itself, which the pious stupidity of the pilgrims identified with the House of Nazareth! Remark seems hardly necessary. The earliest instance of *alma domus* being used as above of the surrounding buildings is in 1447 (ibid., 202).

[84] *Lorette et l'Ultimatum de M. U. Chevalier*, 111–112.

commencement of the present great basilica in 1468. It ran, not from east to west, but from north to south; being thus accommodated to the original arrangement of the Holy House, in which the altar stood in the middle of the southern wall. In it, says Angelita, there still remained the brick wall built around the Holy House, with its pictures of the miraculous translation; and around the church outside there were erected larger porticoes for the shelter of the pilgrims, as well as dwellings for the clergy and a hospital for the sick.

In the middle of the fifteenth century a twofold incident occurred by which the fame of the pilgrimage was much increased: the cure, through the intervention of Our Blessed Lady of Loreto, of two Pontiffs in succession. In 1464 Pope Pius II, after proclaiming a Crusade against the Turks then threatening ruin to all Christendom, experienced the greatest difficulty in arousing the Christian princes from their apathy and had at last formed the heroic resolution of placing himself at the head of the fleet that was gathered at Ancona. A serious illness, however, delayed his setting out from Rome, and in this difficulty he made a vow to Our Blessed Lady of Loreto that if she would obtain his cure, he would go to Loreto with his court and there make an offering of a golden chalice. On this latter he had caused to be inscribed a prayer to Our Lady containing an allusion to "the innumerable signs and miracles" with which she honored her "beloved abode of Loreto" (*Laureti tibi placitam sedem*).

Setting out from Rome with full confidence on June 18, Pius II found his health improve the nearer he approached Loreto. On arriving there, surrounded by his cardinals, he fulfilled his vow to Our Blessed Lady and then proceeded to Ancona, which he reached on July 18, with every promise of at once embarking on the Crusade. Fresh difficulties, however, here awaited him, owing to dissensions among the crusading princes; and the grief caused him by these brought on a return of his disease, of which he died at Ancona on August 14, 1464.

The return of the cardinals to Rome, where was to be held the conclave for the election of his successor, was hastened by an outbreak at Ancona of the plague, with which one member of the Sacred College already was attacked. This was the Venetian Cardinal Pietro Barbo, who, feeling the disease upon him, turned in his distress, as had done the Pontiff just deceased, to Our Lady of Loreto, whither he caused himself to be carried. Being borne into the Holy House itself, he poured out his soul in prayer to Our Blessed Lady, who there appeared to him while he was wrapped in a mysterious sleep, and assuring him that his disease was healed, made known to him his coming election to the Chair of Peter. He came forth from the Holy House completely restored to health, to the amazement of those awaiting him outside; and in his gratitude to Our Blessed Lady he at once sent for the governor of the Holy House and announced to him his intention to erect a great basilica in place of the existing church, directing him at the same time to begin at once the collecting of materials.

In fulfilment of Our Lady's prophecy, only a fortnight after the death of Pius II, Cardinal Barbo was elected to succeed him on August 30, 1464, taking the name of Paul II.

The new Pontiff lost no time in carrying out his intention with reference to Loreto and at once gave orders for the building of the basilica to be commenced. The "oblong" church accordingly was taken down, and so eagerly was the work pressed on that when Paul II died in 1471, the new church, Torsellini thinks, had already almost reached the roof.

The bishop of Recanati at the time of Paul II's accession was Nicholas degli Asti, himself a munificent benefactor to the Santa

Casa. Bishop Asti died, however, on October 7, 1469; and the Pope, the better to ensure the carrying out of his designs with reference to Loreto, did not at once appoint a successor; but, taking the vacant see into his own hands for a while, commissioned the bishop of Parenzo to act as his administrator and to see to the continuation of the work.[85]

It is clear, moreover, that Pope Paul II judged the time to have now arrived when something of the wonders connected with Loreto might be mentioned in official papal utterances, without the reserve his predecessors had observed. Thus, in an encyclical issued on October 19, 1464, less than two months after his election, he not only granted indulgences to those visiting St. Mary of Loreto on the feasts of Our Lady's Assumption, Purification, and Nativity, and on any Sunday, but he made special mention of "the great, stupendous, and well-nigh countless miracles wrought there by the Holy Virgin's means, as *in our own person* we have undoubtedly experienced."

This public declaration of the Pope, as to the miraculous cure wrought in the Holy House upon himself, was thought so important that a summary of the encyclical, from which the above is taken, inscribed upon a marble tablet, was placed upon the wall of the Basilica by Vincent Casali, governor from 1578 to 1580.

More striking still, as alluding to the specially sacred character of the Loreto Sanctuary, are the same Pope's words in a bull of February 12, 1470, in which he granted a Jubilee Indulgence

---

[85] A brief, dated November 2, 1469, in which this arrangement was notified to the Recanati priors, makes plain the fact that the commencement of the basilica was due to the Pope himself, and not, as Vogel and Chevalier wrongly say, to Bishop Asti. Eschbach, *La Vérité Sur le Fait de Lorette*, 296.

to those visiting it during Lent of that year. In this Paul II describes "the church of Blessed Mary of Loreto," as "having been miraculously set down (*miraculose fundatam*) outside the walls of Recanati"; affirming "the same glorious Virgin's image to have been placed in it by a company of the angelic host; as persons who are to be depended on assert, and as the faithful themselves may ascertain."[86]

It is true that in the above the Pope does not expressly name the Holy House as such; but a moment's thought will show us that no mention of the house, as apart from the little church itself, could here be looked for; inasmuch as at the time the Pope refers to (when, namely, it was miraculously set down near Recanati), the "church" consisted solely of the Holy House itself. He is here also silent with reference to the identity of the Loreto House with that of Nazareth, although we cannot doubt his own belief in it. This, as we shall see, he left it to his successors to proclaim.

The enthusiasm excited among the people of Recanati by the granting of this Jubilee indulgence in 1470 is proved by a remarkable document, which Vogel gives in full, and which, as coming from a civic corporation, is probably unique in its kind. It is an invitation, dated only one week later than the papal brief, to come and participate in the graces of the Jubilee, couched by "the Priors and Commune of Recanati" in the form of an encyclical, and addressed "to all and every their Reverend Fathers in

---

[86] Quoted from Paul II by Julius II. Torsellini, who followed an inaccurate version of Paul II's bull, has "Virginis gloriosae *domus et* imago." It is for this that Chevalier unfairly accuses him of interpolation. It has been said already that Paul II's bulls are known only by copies differing somewhat from each other (see ibid., 302–303).

Christ, the Lords Archbishops and Bishops, and to the Illustrious and Exalted Lords of all the States and Countries to whom these letters shall have been presented."

That the civil authorities of a small Italian city should have addressed such an encyclical to the archbishops and bishops and princes of Christendom is an occurrence so unprecedented, remarks Father Eschbach, that "nothing can explain it, except the supposition that the Senate of Recanati was recognized on all sides as holding an exceptional position. No sufficient explanation would be offered by the mere existence in its territory of a chapel, in which it pleased God to work miracles," since the same claim might be made by other corporations without number. "Nothing will explain it," he concludes, "unless the common belief expressed by the writers of the fifteenth century that the Chapel in question actually was the former habitation of the Virgin of Nazareth, who had herself entrusted it to the protection of the Senate by setting it down upon the latter's public road."[87]

The time during which the Jubilee indulgence could be gained had been limited by the Pope, in the first instance, to the Lent of 1470. This was found, however, insufficient to satisfy the crowds of pilgrims who flocked to Loreto desirous of gaining it. Accordingly, a second bull was issued by the Pontiff on January 25 of the next year, renewing the grant of the indulgence for the ensuing Lent of that year, and extending the time for gaining it to the end of Paschal time.

On July 26 of that same year, 1471, Pope Paul II suddenly expired. We may be sure, however, that Our Blessed Lady, who had cured him of the plague, and for whose honor he had shown himself so zealous, did not abandon him in his extremity.

[87] Ibid., 301–302.

Chapter 9

∞

Il Teramano and Blessed Baptist of Mantua

At the period spoken of in the last chapter, the governorship, as it was called, of the Holy House was held by one, of whom, in speaking of Loreto, it would be unpardonable not to make some mention, and who bore the name of Pier Giorgio Tolomei, although known more commonly as Il Teramano, having been born at Teramo in the neighboring province of Abruzzi.

The memory of Teramano is inseparably connected with Loreto, as the author of a brief account of the miraculous translation, which, inscribed in various languages on marble tablets, has remained for centuries affixed to the church walls. Before settling at Loreto in 1430, he had already, in his native city, risen to the dignity of provost of S. Sinideo; but this he renounced to become one of the clergy attached to the service of the Holy House. He was appointed to the governorship of it in 1450, and in that office he continued until his death in the June of 1473.

At the time of his coming to Loreto in 1430, half of the people of the place must have begun life in the preceding century, and must therefore have been able to bear witness to what had been handed down to them by persons living very near the time of the appearance of the Holy House upon their shores. If, then, nothing of the kind had really happened, how impossible it would have been for Teramano (as M. Chevalier apparently would have us think), to have imposed a story of his own invention, not only on all the people of the country, but even on the Popes themselves, whose sanction it successively received—and this, too, without exciting any protest!

It was to him, as governor of the Holy House, that Paul II, on finding himself cured, made known his intention of erecting the basilica; and he is described by Torsellini and other writers as "a man of great integrity and wisdom."

It was, according to the last-named historian, "in the time of Pius II about the year 1460," that Teramano "set up in the House of Loreto for the benefit of the pilgrims a summary of its history, written in a simple and plain style suited to the understanding of the people." This summary of Teramano was written apparently in the first instance upon a tablet of no very strong material and was hung up in the Holy House within reach of the pilgrims, who could take it into their own hands to read. Angelita, who used it in writing his own history only half a century later, describes it as "written in small characters upon a tablet (*tabella*) almost worn-out by age and damp."

He says, however, that printed copies of it were already in circulation in his time; and, in fact, Father Eschbach speaks of no less than four editions of it—"all of them *incunabula*"—which he has found in various libraries. As early also as 1472 (and therefore within Teramano's lifetime), a translation of it in Italian had been published at Florence by Bartholomew, a monk of Vallombrosa, who declared it to have been taken entirely "from the written original in the church of Our Lady of Loreto."[88]

[88] Ibid., 136.

How much Teramano's summary was valued, and how fully the Holy See endorsed the story told in it of the translation, may be judged from the fact that in 1578 Pope Gregory XIII caused it to be engraved in eight languages—namely, Latin, Greek, Arabic, Slavonian, Italian, French, German, and Spanish—on tablets fixed on the walls of the basilica. To these were added later others, in English and in Scotch, the word *Church* being written in the latter *Kirk*.

In spite, however, of the high sanction thus bestowed upon it, Teramano's summary is arbitrarily set aside by M. Chevalier as an invention; it not having, to his mind, he declares, "the tone of a veracious historic document."[89] It is true, indeed, that the style of it is simple and unpolished, and the Latin somewhat unclassical; but much more than this is surely necessary to justify the rejection of a document that has been so solemnly approved.

The story told by Teramano is, of course, the same that we have heard more than once already from Angelita, Torsellini, and the other writers, who appeal to his summary as one of their authorities. The following few extracts from it will therefore here suffice. It begins as follows:

> The church of the Blessed Mary of Loreto was a chamber (*camera*) of the House of the Blessed Virgin Mary, Mother of our Lord Jesus Christ, which House was in the country of Jerusalem of Judea, and in the city of Galilee named Nazareth. In the said chamber the Blessed Virgin Mary was born; there, too, she was brought up, and was saluted later by the Angel Gabriel. In the aforesaid chamber also she nursed her Son Jesus Christ, until He was twelve years

---

[89] Chevalier, *Notre-Dame de Lorette*, 214.

of age.... The Apostles and Disciples consecrated that chamber into a church, and there celebrated the Divine Offices; and Blessed Luke the Evangelist, with his own hands, there made the image to the likeness of the Blessed Virgin Mary, which is there even to the present day.

After relating the translation of the Holy House from Nazareth to Fiume, and from thence to Loreto, and its several changes of place there, Teramano mentions the revelation made in 1296 by Our Lady to the hermit and the sending to Nazareth of the sixteen envoys with its successful result. He then goes on to tell of a vision granted to another hermit, called Paul of the Wood, about ten years before he wrote his summary:

There was here a certain hermit called Brother Paul of the Wood, who lived in a hut in the wood near to this church, and who was every morning in the church for the Divine Office, and was a man of great abstinence and holiness of life. He now has declared that for about ten years, on the day of the Nativity of Mary, which is the 8th day of September, for two hours before daylight, the weather still keeping fine, when he, the said Brother Paul, has come out of his hut and has gone towards the church, he has seen a light descend from the sky upon the aforesaid church, which seemed to be about twelve feet in length and six in breadth, and whilst this light was over the said church it disappeared. For this reason he gave it as his opinion that it was the Blessed Virgin who there appeared on the day of her Nativity. That is what that holy man has seen.

Teramano's summary ends with the depositions of two aged and respected inhabitants of Recanati, which had more than once been made by them to him on oath. These old men must have been well known in the locality when he put up the tablet with his summary in the Holy House; and if the story he declared them to have vouched for had not been already universally believed, he could not have done so without exciting at all events some protest.

The first of these witnesses, named Paolo Renalducci, affirmed, says Teramano, "that his grandfather's grandfather saw the afore-said church, when the angels bore it across the sea, and deposited it in the said wood" and declared that "he, with other persons, had often visited the same church in that wood." The second witness, Francesco Priore, many times declared that "his grandfather, who had lived to the age of a hundred and twenty,[90] told him that he had frequently visited the said church in the said wood."

The same Francesco also affirmed "that his grandfather's grandfather had a house near to the aforesaid church in which he lived, and that in his time it was lifted from the place in the wood by the Angels, and carried on to the hill of the two brothers."[91]

It may be useful to quote the following remark of Dr. North-cote with reference to the testimony of these two witnesses:

It might seem at first sight as if there were a discrepancy between these two witnesses, inasmuch as there is an

---

[90] M. Chevalier, following a defective text of Teramano (as Esch-bach shows on page 134), omits the words "his grandfather," thus making it appear that Francesco himself was 120. The English version of Teramano, translated from the original by Rob. Corbington, S.J., and put up in the basilica in 1634, has, like Father Eschbach's text, "his grandfather being one hundred and twenty years old."

[91] Father Eschbach gives the Latin text of Teramano, with a fac-simile of part of it, from the oldest printed edition in the An-gelica Library at Rome. *La Vérité Sur le Fait de Lorette*, 134.

apparent difference of two generations in the persons who saw the first arrival of the shrine and its removal from the wood to the hill, events which are said to have taken place within a few months of one another; but our author expressly tells us that the grandfather of the second witness lived to the extraordinary age of one hundred and twenty years, so that, in fact, the witnesses were contemporaneous, though of most unequal ages.[92]

Teramano does not name the year in which he took the depositions of the two old men; but if we suppose it to have been even as late as 1460, and the witnesses to have been then each aged eighty, Priore's grandfather (who may easily have lived till about the year 1400) would have been already about fourteen years of age, when the Holy House arrived in 1294; and the great-great-grandfather of Rinalducci may then have been considerably older.

The hermit's vision of the light seen above the Holy House on the feast of Our Lady's Nativity, as told above by Teramano, is mentioned also by Angelita and the other historians of Loreto. It was this, Riera says, that led to the feast of Our Lady's Nativity being from that time observed at Loreto, as its primary feast; and this "with the assent of the Sovereign Roman Pontiffs, by whom great Indulgences were granted on that account."[93]

This apparition of heavenly lights above the Holy House is usually called "the Miracle of the Flames," and was repeated, Torsellini says, during a period extending over many years, and he relates how about twenty years earlier (about 1577),

---

[92] Northcote, *Celebrated Sanctuaries*, 89.
[93] In Martorelli, *Teatro Istorico della Santa Casa*, vol. 1, 54.

diverse citizens of Recanati remarkable for virtue and gravity, reported to Raphael Riera, from whom I received it, that about the day of the Blessed Virgin's Nativity, flames of fire were seen to fall from heaven in the nighttime on the House of Loreto, all the whole city of Recanati looking on; and that they themselves had seen the same many times with exceeding joy of mind; adding withal that the day before the Feast, when it began to be dark, the citizens of Recanati flocked commonly to the houses and walls whence they might behold the House of Loreto, that they might delight their eyes with the admirable beauty of that heavenly flame, which every year was seen (as was reported) until the time of Pope Paul III. Novidius, a famous poet, recorded these events in a notable poem, which he dedicated to Pope Paul III.[94]

Similar apparitions of flames were also sometimes seen, Torsellini tells us, inside the church itself; and he relates an instance of it in 1555, of which Father Riera was himself a witness, who "afterward set down in writing this very thing." On this occasion, while one of the Jesuit Fathers was preaching, "certain bright fires falling down from heaven, in the clear daylight, rested over the most sacred Chapel; then spreading abroad went about the assembled multitude, and then presently into heaven again." Two years later, continues Torsellini,

> when one of the same Fathers was preaching, and some hearing the confessions of pilgrims, suddenly a heavenly flame like unto a comet or blazing star was perceived to glitter and shine, which falling down upon the sacred

---

[94] Torsellini, *History of Loreto*, vol. 1, bk. 1, chap. 17.

Chapel stood there a little while; then going towards the place appointed to hear confessions, moved up and down over the heads of the priests and them that confessed their sins, and finally resting awhile over the image of Christ crucified, which is religiously reverenced in the most sacred Chapel, it mounted again on high, replenishing their hearts with devotion who had seen that heavenly vision.[95]

The last-mentioned especially consoling apparition is also related by Father Renzoli, S.J., who, after noting that it took place upon the feast of Pentecost, exclaims:

Who does not see that by this wonderful favor the Holy Spirit with the splendor of His flames was glorifying the Virgin Mother in that sacred place, in which He had overshadowed her?... And what a pledge this is that those who come to the Virgin's feet, there to lay aside, as does the serpent, the ancient slough of their sins, will obtain pardon, grace, and salvation! Finally, who does not see in this wonderful favor the abundance of gifts which the Holy Spirit is ever ready to impart in this Holy House?[96]

Sixteen years after the death of Teramano, which took place in 1473, Pope Innocent VIII, at the request of Cardinal Jerome della Rovere, then bishop of Recanati, entrusted the care of the Holy House to a band of thirty Carmelite friars, picked men of their order, who entered on their honorable charge in 1489.

They were headed by Blessed Baptist Spagnuoli, surnamed from his place of birth the Mantuan. This holy man, to whom

---

[95] Ibid., bk. 3, chap. 14.

[96] Father Reuzoli's *Santa Casa illustrata e difesa* (1697), given in Martorelli, *Teatro Istorico della Santa Casa*, vol. 2, 343.

in our own days the honors of the Blessed were decreed by Leo XIII, was no less distinguished for his learning than his sanctity, and is famous as a poet; and when he died, in 1516, was the general of his order.

To Blessed Baptist of Mantua we are indebted for several compositions, both in prose and verse, relating to the Holy House; and especially for a brief history of the translation (a paraphrase really of the summary of Teramano with a few additions), of which he gives himself the following account, and which was dedicated by him to Cardinal della Rovere on September 22, 1489.[97]

After speaking of the feeling of sacred fear and awe, with which he had first approached the spot consecrated by so many miracles, Blessed Baptist goes on to say that when, overcoming this first feeling, he set himself to examine the various objects that the holy place contained, his eyes fell upon "a tablet (*tabella*) falling to pieces owing to its (bad) position and its age, on which the history was written explaining whence and how it was that such veneration was claimed for that place." To save the remembrance of so wonderful a thing from being lost, he had determined, he says, "to put together its history from that tablet now almost destroyed by decay and dust."

The historians that followed were unanimous in understanding the decayed tablet, found in the Holy House by Blessed Baptist, to have been the one placed there by Teramano, nor, indeed, was this ever called in question until the middle of the nineteenth century, when an objection was raised by Count Monaldo Leopardi, a nobleman of Recanati, on the ground that the sixteen years between the death of Teramano and the coming to Loreto of the Carmelites were insufficient to account for the

---

[97] Blessed Baptist's history is also given in Martorelli, vol. 1.

decayed state of the tablet, conceiving this, as he did, to have been made of solid wood.[98]

We have seen, however, that Angelita, who made use of Teramano's summary, describes it as "*written* in small characters"; and therefore, apparently, not on wood, but only on parchment or thick paper.

The fact that Blessed Baptist's composition is in reality but a paraphrase of Teramano's summary put into more elegant Latin has been made quite clear by Father Eschbach, who prints the two, side by side, in parallel columns. It is true that the account of Blessed Baptist contains a few additions to it; but these, as he says himself, are very few, and "in no way at variance with the story found (by him) on the tablet." Of these additions we need only note his mention, as then "still existing" in the Holy House, of the "wooden Cross placed there by the Apostles in remembrance of the Passion of our Lord." Although not spoken of by Teramano, this cross, as we have seen, is mentioned expressly by the Tersatto writers, as also in the Macerata judgment of 1315; and according to the traditions both of Tersatto and Loreto, it was placed in the Holy House by the Apostles.

It may be well, however, to take notice of what seems at first a discrepancy between the accounts of Teramano and Blessed Baptist, with reference to the hermit Paul; the former represents the hermit as having related to himself the vision of the flames;

---

[98] On the strength of this, and other equally futile objections to be mentioned later, Leopardi, while maintaining the truth of the translation of the Holy House from Nazareth, struck out an extravagant theory of his own, to the effect that its removal from Nazareth had taken place at some much earlier period; and that it had been kept concealed by God, until the time for it to be made known in Europe came.

whereas the second writer seems to refer their apparition to the time—a century and a half earlier—when the Holy House was in the wood. This seeming discrepancy is explained by Father Eschbach as due simply to the poetic style of Blessed Baptist, which led him (mistakenly, as it would seem) to transpose some clauses of Teramano's simpler narrative.

It is really painful to remark that this saintly and learned Carmelite fares at the hands of M. Chevalier in the same way as the other upholders of the Loreto tradition. His straightforward narrative is set down by the Canon as "a rhapsody"; and, worse still, he even ventures to insinuate that "he may not have been too holy to assert what was untrue." "The legendary character of this History," he writes, "is accentuated by the fact that the Mantuan gives all the merit of the building of Loreto Church to Cardinal della Rovere;... and that he passes over in silence the initiative and the gifts of Bishop Nicholas degli Asti."[99]

With reference to this latter point, it is true that Bishop Asti, acting under Pope Paul II, took part in the beginning of the work; but since he died not long after its commencement, and nineteen years before the coming of the Carmelites, there seems to have been no call for Blessed Baptist to make any special mention of him in the book in question. On the other hand, in dedicating his little book to Cardinal della Rovere, at whose invitation the Carmelites had come to Loreto, it was only fitting that Blessed Baptist should make in it a suitable acknowledgment of his zeal in carrying on the work. That the chief part in this had fallen to the cardinal is only what Riera, Torsellini, and the other Loreto historians all agree in saying. In this we have another instance of the flimsiness of the objections advanced against the Loreto writers.

[99] Chevalier, *Notre-Dame de Lorette*, 250–252.

The House of the Virgin Mary

At the end of his account of the Holy House and its basilica, Blessed Baptist relates a noteworthy incident of which he was himself a witness on July 16, 1489. "I will not pass over," he says, "a thing which I saw with my own eyes and heard with my own ears.... It happened that a French lady of some means and of gentle birth named Antonia, who had long been possessed by several evil spirits, was brought into the holy place by her husband that she might be delivered. Whilst a priest named Stephan, an exemplary man, was reading over her the usual exorcisms, one of the demons, who gave himself the name of Arctus, and who boasted that he had been the instigator of the massacre of all the Innocents, being asked to his confusion whether this had been the Immaculate Virgin's chamber, replied that it had been so indeed, but that he owned it against his will, compelled by Mary to confess the truth. He moreover pointed to the places (in the Holy House) where Gabriel, and where Mary, had each of them been. Being further adjured to say who had had charge of the place itself when it was in Nazareth, after repeated exorcisms … he at length unwillingly replied that the ancient Carmelites had had the charge of it."[100]

This incident is also told by Angelita, whose father, he says, was present at it, as well as by Riera and Torsellini. From these we learn that the northeast corner of the Holy House — namely, the gospel side of the present altar, but in the part known as the Santo Camino — was the place pointed out as occupied at the Annunciation by Our Lady, that of the Angel being nearer to the other end of the house, on the right side of the window.[101]

---

[100] Translated from the text as in ibid., 247.
[101] Martorelli, *Teatro Istorico della Santa Casa*, vol. 1, 62, 190, 528.

Chapter 10

Alterations Made by Clement VII

The great basilica begun by Paul II, within which the Holy House has stood since then enshrined, was completed by Julius II, Pope from 1503 to 1513, by whom also were erected the fortifications, intended to protect the Sanctuary from the Turks or other foes, which give it somewhat of the appearance of a castle. At the far end also of the noble square this same Pope commenced the building of the papal palace, which, designed by Bramante, the great architect of St. Peter's, and majestically facing the basilica, by the mere fact of its presence there proclaims the Roman Pontiff's recognition of the peculiarly sacred character of the Sanctuary.

Pope Leo X, who succeeded Julius in 1513, spared no pains to carry out the unfulfilled intentions of his predecessor with reference to the adornment of the Holy House. It was from him that Sansovino received his commission to design the beautiful encasement of Carrara marble now encircling it, which, however, was not actually erected in the lifetime of Pope Leo, as the carving of it, with its innumerable bas-reliefs and statues, was a work of many years.

The erection of it took place under Pope Clement VII. Before continuing the work, this Pontiff, says Riera, dispatched messengers to Loreto, to Tersatto, and to Nazareth, charged to collect additional information "as to what had taken place in those localities in connection with the Sanctuary at Loreto." "One of these messengers," adds Riera, "was a special friend of mine, and from him I received an account of the whole matter." The report of these messengers as to the wonders by which the Holy House had been glorified in the places above mentioned determined the Pope, "not only to carry on the work (of its adornment), but also to honor it in other striking ways."[102] A fuller account of the incident is given us by Torsellini, who says that the commissioners sent upon this embassy were three of the Pope's chamberlains. First going to Loreto, they took there the measurements of the Holy House; then proceeding to Tersatto, they there examined the chapel built upon the spot where it had rested, as well as the inscriptions recording its coming and departure. Finally, at Nazareth, they found the Loreto measurements to correspond exactly with those of the foundations there remaining. One, moreover, of the envoys, a certain John of Siena, brought back with him two specimens of the Nazareth stone. On returning to Loreto they compared these with the stones of the Holy House, and found them to be of the same kind.[103]

One of the most laborious, though at the same time most beneficial, works of Clement VII was the drying up of the swampy marshes at the foot of the Loreto hill, from which pestilential vapors rose; as also the levelling at great cost of two hillocks that prevented the circulation of the wind. Until this was done, so insalubrious, indeed, had been the place that several of the Carmelite Fathers, who had been put in charge of it, had died;

[102] Riera, *History of Loreto*, 148.
[103] Ibid., 207.

and the survivors, greatly to their regret, had been recalled elsewhere by their superiors in 1498.

The setting up of the marble incrustation of the Holy House
was commenced in 1531. The doors at the two ends of the House,
of which the Nazareth pilgrims speak, had been built up before
its translation from the east; and at the time we speak of, the
only door into it was the one in the middle of the north side,
which at Nazareth must have led into the cave. It is easy to
understand the inconveniences of this arrangement, and the
confusion necessarily caused by the struggles of the pilgrims all
passing in and out through this one door; which was, moreover,
in a special manner sacred, as having been used by the members of the Holy Family. Pope Clement VII, therefore, ordered
this ancient doorway to be built up, with materials obtained by
the opening of two new doorways for the entrance and exit of
the people on the north and south sides. At the same time, he
ordered the outline of the builtup doorway to be retained upon
the wall, as is still to be seen.

The altar also, which then stood on the south side and opposite the door, was by him moved to the east end, as seen at
present;[104] and a third doorway was opened by his order, giving
access to the space between the east wall and the altar, which
is looked upon as the most sacred portion of the Holy House.

It seems that this portion at the east end of the house was
originally partitioned off, so as to form a separate room; and it thus
appears to answer to the "chamber without light," mentioned by
Phocas as the one in which our Lord is said to have lived. Riera

---

[104] The original altar consecrated by St. Peter was placed within
the modern one, through a grating in the front of which it can
be seen when the antependium is raised.

has much to say as to the favors received there by devout suppliants, of which he had been himself a witness. "It was there," he says, "according to the tradition of our elders that the most Blessed Virgin Mary actually was, when she was saluted by the Angel and became the Mother of God."[105] There, in a niche raised high enough to be seen above the reredos of the altar, is the image of Our Lady carved by St. Luke, adorned with precious jewels that shine like little stars in the light of the many lamps.

A blackened recess in the wall below the image, which at one time was taken for a fireplace, has caused this part of the house behind the altar to be called the Santo Camino, or Sacred Hearth. Father Hutchison, however, was convinced that the recess was really but a closed-up doorway. The so-called Camino, which was put into its present form only in the time of Clement VII, has, he says, no real shaft or chimney. Chimneys are, moreover, rare in Palestine, and in Nazareth he thinks there is not even one.

The carrying out of these bold alterations was marked by an alarming incident, which Riera says was related to him by Nerucci, the architect to whom it happened. To many people it seemed almost an impiety to break open the walls of the Holy House in the way required for the three new doorways; and in consequence of this strong feeling it was determined to execute the work by night. Accordingly, on the evening of May 11, 1531, Nerucci, with a band of workmen, came, says Riera, prepared to make the openings.

Having traced the outline of one doorway in the place intended, he struck the wall with his hammer, calling

[105] Martorelli, *Teatro Istorico della Santa Casa*, vol. 1, 146.

at the same time to the workmen: "Make the opening here." Instantly a fit of trembling seized his arm, and his heart no longer beating he sank upon the ground; and thinking he was going to die, he recalled his order to the workmen, and was carried almost lifeless home and laid upon his bed. Having implored Our Lady of Loreto's help, he received from God the restoration of his health, and when sufficiently recovered reported what had happened to the Pope.[106]

With the above, Riera's unfinished *History of Loreto* abruptly ends, but the remainder of the architect's story is told by Torsellini. The Pope, in spite of this occurrence, insisted that the work be continued; and he tried to encourage Nerucci not to be afraid to go on with what had been ordered by God's vicar. At the same time, understanding that this punishment had been brought upon Nerucci by his overconfidence and want of reverence, the Pope warned him to prepare himself with fasting and devout acts of veneration toward the Holy Virgin. Nerucci, however, now showed himself as timid as he had before been bold and would not be persuaded to make the attempt a second time. The work thus remained at a standstill, until a young cleric named Ventura Perini, relying on the Pope's authority, offered himself to do what was required. After fasting, therefore, for three days, this young ecclesiastic reverently approached the Holy House and, falling on his knees, first uttered a prayer aloud; then rising struck the wall with his hammer without any evil consequence. He was followed by the workmen, who were also fasting, and thus the three doors were opened.

---

[106] Riera, *History of Loreto*, 150.

The House of the Virgin Mary

The erection of the marble casing was not begun until November 1531, for it had been necessary first to build around the Holy House a wall strong enough to support the new encasement, and resting on firm foundations; and for this purpose the wall, which had been erected around it on its first arrival, had to be taken down. On this latter wall pictures, it will be remembered, had been painted exhibiting the various removals of the Holy House; and these pictures, which Angelita speaks of as still existing in his time, had now unfortunately to be destroyed. The remembrance of them is preserved, however, by two bas-reliefs at the east end of the new encasement representing the same scenes.

To this same period also belongs the stone roof, which now covers the Holy House and which rests on the new wall supporting the encasement. Clement VII ordered the old wooden roof to be taken down, for fear it should someday catch fire from the many lamps and candles, and the planks of which it had consisted were laid beneath the predella of the altar.

We have seen that the accounts of the Holy House that have reached us, both from Tersatto and Loreto, all from the first describe it as standing on the ground without foundations. The truth of this fact was placed beyond all doubt during the carrying out of the changes above mentioned. For Riera says that he was assured by many, who themselves had been present at the digging of the foundations for the new encasing wall, that the workmen found the Holy House itself to be resting simply on the surface of the ancient road, some of the dust of which they actually took from underneath its walls. The same persons, moreover, declared that in the taking down of the old surrounding wall, this was found to be so entirely detached from the house itself that a boy with a lighted candle had been able to pass all around between it and the house, thus making it plain that the latter had nothing to support it but the loose earth of the road on which it stood.[107] The fact, indeed, of there being no foundations to it has since been verified in modern times.

It was found necessary in the middle of the eighteenth century to renew the marble pavement of the Holy House. When permission for this was requested from Pope Benedict XIV, he made it a condition that the foundation of the walls should be carefully examined in presence of competent witnesses. The taking up of the old pavement was begun on April 14, 1751, three architects and four master masons having been engaged to examine the lower portions of the walls thus laid bare, and the proceedings being conducted in the presence, not only of the diocesan bishop of Recanati and Loreto, but also of the archbishop of Fermo and of the neighboring bishops of Jesi, Ascoli, and Macerata. The attestation signed by these prelates and by the seven architects and master masons on April 23, 1751, is preserved in the archives of the Santa Casa. In it they declare on oath that "from the altar steps to the opposite end of the Holy House, which they have carefully examined, there is no foundation of any kind whatever to its sacred walls; that under the walls there is artificially made earth (*terra smossa*), and in some places dust, with little bits of broken stone, and the natural tufa found in mountainous districts."

There is also preserved a letter, written on the night of April 22, on which the examination had been finished, by Don Antonio Lucidi, archdeacon of Loreto, in which he says that the earth underneath the walls was found to be so light and dry that openings were easily scraped through it to the outside of the walls

---

[107] Ibid., 149.

by the workmen's hands alone, and that through one of these openings he himself had passed his arm. Through these openings also it was clearly seen, he says, "not only that the sacred walls stood on no foundations, but also that they received no support from the wall to which the marble is affixed, this being quite separated from them." Don Lucidi tells us also that, during the time that these excavations were still open, they were examined, not only by those already mentioned as having signed the official attestation, but also by members of the chapter, the magistrates of the town, the superiors of the religious orders, and the chaplains and penitentiaries of the basilica.[108]

In making the attestation above given, the bishops note especially how completely their own observation had confirmed the statement, as to the absence of foundations, inscribed upon the marble tablet erected in 1595 at the east end of the Holy House by order of Pope Clement VIII.[109] The same also applies, of course, to the still earlier tablets containing the account of Teramano, in which the same fact is asserted.

The fact, therefore, that the Holy House stands without foundations is established beyond the reach of doubt. Let us now see what writers have further to tell us as to its foundations left at Nazareth.

We have already heard how its earliest historians relate that these were found and verified at Nazareth by the envoys from Tersatto, as well as by those from Piceno, sent in 1296.

We have also seen how the same was confirmed by the envoys sent by Clement VII. Speaking of the Piceno envoys of 1296: "These," says Teramano, "carried with them the measurements

---

[108] See Eschbach, *La Vérité Sur le Fait de Lorette*, 217, 221.
[109] See pp. 15–16 of this book.

of the said church, and there discovered the foundations of the said church, the measurements of which answered exactly to the same." "There is," he continues, "an inscription on the opposite wall saying that this church *was* there, and afterwards vanished."

On the strength of this last sentence, M. Chevalier attempts to discredit Teramano, representing him as asserting that the Recanati envoys themselves saw the abovementioned inscription.[110] It is, indeed, easy to see that such Christians as may have been left at Nazareth in 1296 cannot have been in a position to put up any inscription of that kind, nor does Teramano really say so. On the other hand, both Angelita and Riera tell us that neither the Tersatto nor the Recanati envoys, had contrived to get there, excepting at the risk of their lives, and protected by a hired escort. Teramano must therefore be understood to be speaking of an inscription placed there later, of which he may easily have been informed by pilgrims, since the Knights of St. John were allowed by Tamerlane, in 1403, at least temporarily to restore the Christian monuments at Nazareth.

As to the fact that the pilgrims to Palestine of the fifteenth century came back proclaiming the translation of the Holy House from Nazareth to Loreto, we have the testimony of Jerome di Raggiolo, a monk of Vallombrosa and contemporary of Teramano. Raggiolo says with reference to Loreto: "That this is the chamber … into which, at Nazareth in Galilee, the Angel Gabriel was sent … to the Virgin Mary, all are unanimous in asserting who from devotion travel to Jerusalem."

The work of Raggiolo, from which this is taken, was written at the latest in 1479, in which year died Francesco Altovita,

[110] Chevalier, *Notre-Dame de Lorette*, 251.

whom its author mentions as the general of the Vallombrosa Order at the time he wrote.

M. Chevalier attempts to weaken the force of this striking testimony by sneeringly remarking that its author is shown by his works to have been "more pious than critical." Even so, his word must still be taken as to what the pilgrims of his time declared; and Raggiolo's value as an author may be estimated from the praises bestowed on him by such writers as Ruinart and Mabillon, and from the fact that in their great *Acta Sanctorum* the Bollandists thought it worthwhile to transcribe a great portion of his works.

In support, moreover, of his statement as to the translation of the Holy House, Eschbach quotes the testimony of a pilgrim of that very time, which Chevalier has failed to notice — that, namely, of William Landgrave of Hesse, who, on his way back from the Holy Land, went to Loreto in 1483 and who speaks of the translation of the Holy House, and of the discovery at Nazareth of its foundations, as a then already well-known fact.[111]

It is true, indeed, that, during the two first centuries after the translation, few of the pilgrims to Nazareth make actual mention in their written accounts of the disappearance of the Holy House, and that for the most part they speak only of what they found still there. But it is important to take notice that M. Chevalier is able to produce only one writer of the fifteenth century whose account is in reality at variance with the tradition of Loreto. Moreover, this one opponent of it, Suriano, himself admits the currency of that tradition, which he attacks, as we shall see, under the mistaken

[111] Eschbach, *La Vérité Sur le Fait de Lorette*, 124.

notion that the Loreto House is built not of stone but brick. All this shows that M. Chevalier is quite wrong in placing at 1508 the first Nazareth testimony to Loreto. After that date, however, he himself admits the practical unanimity of the Nazareth pilgrims in asserting the translation.

The truth of the tradition as to the finding of the foundations of the Holy House at Nazareth has been placed beyond the reach of doubt by the investigations there made by the Franciscans in 1620. The then prince of Saida (Sidon), Fachr-ed-Din, within whose dominion Nazareth was included, was very friendly to the Christians. Some years before, he had for a time been driven from his throne, but had been most kindly received in Italy by Pope Paul V, and on being restored to his dominions, he showed his gratitude by making over to the Franciscans, at the request of Father Thomas of Novara, their superior, the Sanctuary of the Annunciation, which they have ever since retained.

On taking possession of it, the Franciscans found the whole place in ruins, except a chapel in the crypt, called the Chapel of the Angel, which had been built upon the site once occupied by the Holy House. This chapel was supposed by them at first to be a replica of it, and Thomas of Novara, who had brought from Loreto a plan of the Holy House, with its dimensions marked upon it, was disturbed on finding those of the chapel to be considerably less. Being obliged, however, to leave Nazareth for a time and to go to Jerusalem, he left the work of making excavations to be carried on meantime by Father James of Vendome.

The excavations conducted by Vendome resulted, to Novara's relief, in the discovery that only a part of the site on which the Holy House had stood was covered by the Chapel of the Angel, the southern and western walls of which had had to be taken down on account of their decayed condition. Their removal had brought to light the foundations of the Holy House, which on those two sides lay outside the walls of the chapel.

On his return to Europe shortly after, Thomas of Novara published an account of the discovery, from which we take the following:

> Leaving then the foundations of this later structure (namely, of the Chapel of the Angel), and returning to the true and primitive foundations, we drew the measuring-line from these, and to the joy of all we satisfied ourselves that the dimensions of the Sanctuary of Nazareth agreed in every respect with those which we found marked upon the plan of the Holy House of Loreto. And we found that the foundations entirely agreed, and were commensurate with the walls, and the House with the foundations, and the place with the place, the site with the site, and the space with the space, at Nazareth and Loreto — that foundation I have spoken of being removed.[112]

Novara then goes on to mention a thing "unknown," he says, "till then to anyone" — namely, that the doorway built up at Loreto exactly answers to the one by which the cave is now entered at Nazareth. "Each is at the same distance from the angles, is of the same form, and is placed there for the same purpose — namely, to give access, not to the House, but to the grotto.... Each also looks to the north." In his gratitude to God for having thus solved the doubts that had been troubling him, Novara exclaims: "Now, that which for years has been sought for, by some out of religious

---

[112] Taken from ibid., 469, and Hutchison, *Loreto and Nazareth*, 75. Novara's *De recuperatione sacrae Domus Annuntiationis* was printed in Venice in 1623.

zeal, by others out of curiosity, or wish to learn the truth, has thus in our days been proved and remains clearer than the sun."[113]

The learned Francis Quaresmius, whom Eschbach calls "the Prince of Palestinographers," was himself a witness of this discovery of the foundations by Novara; the accuracy of whose account he attested, embodying it in 1639 in his great work *Elucidatio Terra Sanctae*.

The fact, therefore, that the foundations of the Holy House had been left at Nazareth, and were there seen in 1620, just as they had been seen centuries before by the envoys from Tersatto and Piceno, is established without room for doubt.

Unfortunately, in the hurried building of the present church in 1730 (the completion of which within three months was insisted upon by the Turks),[114] the foundations were again put out of sight, although the line along which ran the south wall of the Holy House is still indicated by two slabs of black marble fixed in the wall of the staircase leading down into the Chapel of the Angel.[115] We must hope that the completion of the excavations begun some years ago may once more bring to light the actual foundations.

---

[113] Eschbach, *La Vérité Sur le Fait de Lorette*, 471.

[114] During those three months the Musulmans made their pilgrimage to Mecca. Eschbach, *Lorette et l'Ultimatum de M. U. Chevalier*, 47–48.

[115] Father Vlaminck's *Report of the Excavations*, given by Abbe Faurax, *L'abbé J. Faurax*, vol. 4, 87.

Chapter 11

∽

The Materials of Which
the Holy House Is Built

We have seen that the pilgrims to Palestine of the fifteenth century are said to have been well-nigh unanimous, on their return, in asserting that the Holy House no longer was at Nazareth, but had been removed to Loreto; and even M. Chevalier finds himself obliged to acknowledge the general acceptance of the "legend," as he calls it, toward the beginning of the following century. Indeed, two writers only, one of the fifteenth and the other of the sixteenth century, are able to be quoted by him as bearing testimony against the tradition; and these two are shown in each case to have based their disbelief in it upon mistaken information as to the materials of which the Holy House is constructed.

The first of these opponents was the Franciscan already mentioned, Francesco Suriano, who wrote a treatise on the Holy Land in 1485. In this, in speaking of Nazareth, he expressed himself as follows: "Some have falsely said that the House in which she (Our Lady) dwelt, and in which she was announced by the Angel, is St. Mary's of Loreto, which is made of bricks or tiles (*quadreli o matoni*), and is covered with tiles (*copi*), whereas in this country such things are not found."[116]

The second opponent was a French knight, Greffin Affagard, who, after making the pilgrimage to Nazareth, put forward, in 1533, a like statement as to the materials of the Holy House (perhaps suggested by Suriano's book), and on that ground protested, like him, against the tradition with reference to Loreto.[117]

M. Chevalier naturally makes much of these two protests. Whatever force, however, they might otherwise have had, disappears in face of the fact that the ground of their objection has been proved to be mistaken; while their very protests against the Loreto tradition are themselves a proof of the widespread acceptance of it. In fact, Suriano, in an imaginary dialogue with his sister, makes her say that *everyone* believed in the miraculous translation. Suriano is not known ever to have visited Loreto, and his rashness in speaking as he did about the materials of the Holy House has been remarked upon even by members of his own order.[118]

Nevertheless, the same erroneous opinion as to the materials has been more than once expressed in modern times, and the appearance of the walls themselves of the Holy House gives at first sight some countenance to it, till they are carefully examined. "It has been asserted by some," says Father Hutchison,

> that the walls were built of brick. This, however, is not the case. People were misled by the reddish tint, and by the fact that the stone were of a narrow brick-like form, not unlike the shape of the Roman bricks; but it was

[116] Chevalier, *Notre-Dame de Lorette*, 69, 236.
[117] Ibid., 78.
[118] Eschbach, *La Vérité Sur le Fait de Lorette*, 459.

pointed out that the stones could not be bricks, because bricks are made in a mold and are therefore all of the same size, whereas these stones were of different sizes and thickness.[119]

In the middle of last century, a scientific examination was made, both of the Loreto materials, and of those of buildings at Nazareth, which ought to put the question entirely at rest. Difficulties against the identity of the Loreto House with that of Nazareth had been raised by Dean Stanley in his *Sinai and Palestine*. He admitted, indeed, that the Loreto House was not of brick, but he described its material as "a dark red polished stone wholly unlike anything in Palestine," all the buildings there being "of the natural grey limestone of the country."[120] At the request of Cardinal Wiseman, a special examination of these difficulties raised by Stanley was made by Monsignor (afterward Cardinal) Bartolini, who was then about to make a pilgrimage to Nazareth, and who obtained from Pope Pius IX permission to remove for the purpose from the Holy House small portions both of the stones and of the mortar, in order to submit them to chemical analysis.

As to the reddish color, observed by Dean Stanley, on the stones *inside* the Holy House (for those on the outside are concealed from view by the encasement): "It is true," says Father Hutchison,

> that there is a dark reddish tint over the greater part of the walls, and some care is necessary to ascertain the real

[119] Hutchison, *Loreto and Nazareth*, 78.
[120] Dean Stanley, *Sinai and Palestine* (1856), 443–450. Dean Stanley's difficulty as to the *one* door has been met already by showing that there were originally others at the ends of the Holy House.

color of the stones. The fact is, that from age, and from the smoke of the lamps perpetually burning in the Holy House, the stones have become in most places almost black and from the kisses of the pilgrims they have become, at least to a certain height, quite polished.

He goes on to explain that the reddish tint they show is due to the mortar made from "the red volcanic stone of the neighborhood," with which, in the time of Clement VII, the walls were pointed, in order to fill up interstices between the stones, and so to hinder these from being easily pulled out.

The result of Msgr. Bartolini's investigations as to the physical nature of the stones themselves was in the highest degree satisfactory. In addition to the stones and mortar obtained by him at Loreto, he brought back with him from Nazareth specimens of its stones and mortar, extracted, partly from the cave in front of which the Holy House had stood, partly from ancient buildings in the town.

On his return to Rome he sent two specimens of the stones of each place—enclosed in separate packets and with nothing to indicate from whence they severally came—to the professor of chemistry at the Sapienza University, Dr. Francesco Ratti, with a request that he would analyze them. Father Hutchison gives in full Professor Ratti's report of his analysis, as published in 1861 by Msgr. Bartolini. It will be enough for our purpose to quote here the conclusion. "Having taken," the Professor says,

> a portion from each of the four specimens, and submitted it to chemical analysis, it turns out that they are *all of the same nature*, being all formed of carbonate of lime, carbonate of magnesia, and ferruginous clay. If it happens that in any of the specimens there is a difference, as for example

... a little more clay and iron, this difference does not alter the nature of the stone, and depends on conditions which are absolutely secondary, on the fortuitous aggregation of different quantities of the same materials.

The result of this analysis is to make it plain, writes Father Hutchison, "that the stone of which the Holy House of Loreto is composed is limestone *identical with that of Nazareth*, the stone about Loreto being of a totally different character. The natural stone in that neighborhood is in fact a red volcanic stone."

Equally significant was the result of the analysis of the ancient mortar of the Holy House, which

was found to consist of lime, or chalk, worked up with some small pieces of vegetable charcoal ... very different from the cement used in Italy. The ancient mortar, then, as well as the stone, came to Loreto from afar, and was of precisely the same nature as that now found in Palestine.[121]

This last discovery, with reference to the mortar, effectually disposes of the suggestion put forward by some, to the effect that the House at Loreto might have been built up, where it stands, of stones brought there from Nazareth. This suggestion, in addition to its resting purely on conjecture with no facts to support it, would require us to suppose that, not only the stones, but the mortar also, had been brought from Nazareth!

On "the plea that his book has already grown to too great a size" (although he has found room in it for innumerable things of less importance), M. Chevalier excuses himself from giving any

---

[121] Hutchison, *Loreto and Nazareth*, 70–84.

extracts from Cardinal Bartolini's book or the report of Professor Ratti. And he dismisses the matter (in a way that we do not know what to term but flippant) by remarking that he has been assured by "two scientific friends of his at Rome," whose names he does not mention, that "*le brave Bartolini* was mistaken in what he had been told as to the resemblance between the stones of Nazareth and Loreto"![122]

If one of the Loreto writers, on whom Canon Chevalier is so severe, had so acted with reference to a scientific analysis, what would he have said?

Scarcely less unsatisfactory is his mode of referring to an examination of the walls of the Holy House that was made, he says, in July of 1905, on the part of a member of the Görres-Gesellschaft. "The results of it," he announces, "will be given to the public without delay."[123]

No such report appearing, a second reference, says Father Eschbach, was made to the matter by M. Chevalier, in the *Ami du Clerge* of 1908, in which he stated that "in July 1905, Dr. Schaeffer of the Görres-Gesellschaft had examined the walls of the Chapel of Loreto, and had concluded formally against the legend."[124] Nevertheless, how little had been done on this occasion, which could have really led to any such conclusion, may be seen, says Father Eschbach, from the account of the proceeding in the *Annals of the Santa Casa*, for December 1906. Dr. Schaeffer had been aided by a civil engineer, a master mason, and seven other commissioners, who, after satisfying themselves that the walls, to the height of about three meters, were composed of

---

[122] Chevalier, *Notre-Dame de Lorette*, 453.

[123] Ibid., 478.

[124] Quoted by Eschbach, *La Vérité Sur le Fait de Lorette*, 231.

stones — the upper layers above that height (namely, the layers added at Loreto) being formed of bricks — took with them into the sacristy, to be there examined in the daylight, some fragments gathered from the walls, together with a specimen of the cement picked from beneath one of the stones. After examining them merely with the naked eye, and without any attempt at chemical analysis, they agreed in pronouncing "the stones to be reddish and very hard, and the cement to contain charcoal." The specimens were then deposited by them in the Santo Camino, the whole investigation not having occupied two hours.

No official report of the examination had as yet been published when Father Eschbach's second work appeared as late as 1915.

It seems safe, then, to conclude that the examination, such as it was, made by Dr. Schaeffer in 1905 had not resulted really in any discovery at variance with the conclusions of Cardinal Bartolini and Professor Ratti.[125]

The latest attack upon the Holy House has consisted in a futile attempt to show that the stones of which it is constructed are in reality of the same composition as those now obtained from the quarries of the neighboring promontory of Monte Conero.

The defenders of this new suggestion do not pretend to ground it on any chemical analysis; and, indeed — although M. Chevalier was led apparently to think the contrary — the Florence periodical,[126] in which it was propounded, expressly stated that no such analysis had been made.

[125] Ibid., 232. The futility of Dr. Schaeffer's proceeding is fully confirmed by the report of it given by Signor Gianuizzi, the official archivist of Loreto, who himself was present. *Lorette et l'Ultimatum de M. U. Chevalier*, 63.

[126] *La Rassegna Nazionale*, September 1, 1907.

The House of the Virgin Mary

It is true that the stones of Monte Conero do bear some external resemblance in color, and in the shape into which they naturally divide, to the stones of the Holy House; but that the resemblance, such as it is, is only external, and that they are essentially different in composition, is made certain by the experiments to which Father Eschbach has caused them to be subjected, an account of which he gives in his latest work.

Having obtained the requisite permission, Father Eschbach took from the Holy House specimens of the two kinds of stone found in its walls and sent them for analysis, as well as specimens of the Monte Conero stone, to Dr. X, whom he describes as "one of the most celebrated of European chemists." The specimens were conveyed to the latter, not together, but at intervals of a month, and with no indication of the source from which they were obtained.

The report found that, while the stone of Monte Conero contained but four elements, each of those of the Holy House contained eight or nine. This analysis, says Father Eschbach, completes without contradicting that of Professor Ratti, since whose time the art of chemical science has made great advance, other simple bodies having been discovered.

Father Eschbach expresses his regret that, in spite of repeated efforts, he has been unable, owing to the present war, to obtain specimens of the stones of Nazareth to submit to a like analysis. The above, however, suffices to show that the stones of the Holy House were not procured from the promontory of Monte Conero.

This chapter may fitly be concluded by relating how the conversion of an Anglican clergyman to the Catholic Faith was brought about by his study of the materials of the Holy House.

The clergyman in question, Dr. Faller, a tutor of the University of Oxford, was very eager to convict the Church of Rome of serious error on some point of liturgy, and being in Palestine about the year 1858, he thought he saw an opportunity of doing so in connection with the office of the translation of the Holy House. Accordingly, having provided himself with a store of instruments and chemical ingredients, he set out for Nazareth. On reaching the Sanctuary of the Incarnation, he set himself to make innumerable scientific experiments, measuring with incredible minuteness, within and without, from above and below, and again from below upward, whatever traces remain of the ancient abode of the Holy Family. He decomposed and analyzed materials, and at last, when this laborious work was done, he embarked for Italy and went straight to Loreto. There he recommenced the same operations, comparing the results with those obtained at Nazareth. Then perceiving that he still lacked certain indications, he went back to Galilee, and thence again to Loreto. But lo! the more closely he continued his investigation, the more did his prejudices give way to confusion, and his confusion to contrition, and this last to conversion. He went back for the third time to Nazareth, no longer as a chemist, but as a Catholic believer.[127]

[127] Quoted in ibid., 54., from the account given in *Annales de la Mission de Notre Dame de Sion, annee 1858*, by "Marie Ratisbonne" (apparently Father Mary Alphonsus Ratisbonne, miraculously converted in Rome in 1842 by an apparition of Our Lady).

Chapter 12

Papal Utterances with Reference to Loreto

The question as to the authenticity of the Holy House being one so closely connected with religion, the utterances of the Popes on the subject ought necessarily to be to Catholics of paramount importance, both on account of the supreme authority attached to the verdict of Christ's Vicar, and of the special guidance believed ordinarily to attend his action; to say nothing of the proverbial caution observed in his pronouncements.

This being so well understood by Catholics, we cannot but regard it as surprising that critics of Loreto, such as Canon Chevalier and his supporters, should show themselves apparently quite ready to admit that, in the matter now before us, Pontiff after Pontiff has not only allowed himself to be disgracefully deceived, but actually has done his best to foster and encourage an untrue belief.

The pronouncements of the Pontiffs with reference to Loreto (some of which have been already quoted) have been indeed so numerous that only the more important ones can be repeated here. In these the reader will not fail to note that, in accordance with the well-known practice of the Holy See, the first utterances are very cautious in their language, while those that follow grow more and more explicit, as the fact of the miraculous translation was more and more confirmed.

M. Chevalier tries to make some capital out of the *tardiness* with which, as he conceives, the Pontiffs gave their approbation to the belief in the translation; but to the right-minded Catholic, papal sanction, whether granted late or early, ought to carry the same weight; and if, in the case in question, there was unusual delay, the peculiar difficulties attached to the time and circumstances seem sufficiently to explain it, as the following facts will show.

Pope Nicholas IV, toward the close of whose pontificate the Holy House made its appearance at Tersatto, died within a year of its arrival. On his death in April 1292, a vacancy of more than two years ensued, followed by the five months' pontificate of St. Peter Celestine, who abdicated on December 13, 1294, only three days after the removal of the Holy House into Italy. Then came the troubled pontificate of Boniface VIII, in continual contest with the rebellious Colonnas and Philip the Fair of France, and ending with the outrage on the Pontiff at Anagni, which cost him his life in 1303. Then, when Blessed Benedict XI had reigned for but eight months, there came another long vacancy, followed by the removal of the Popes to Avignon for seventy years, Italy being torn meanwhile between the factions of the Guelfs and the Ghibellines. Then — worse still — from 1378 to 1417 came the great Schism of the West.

Under such circumstances it need not surprise us that, for the first hundred years after the arrival of the Holy House at Loreto, there should not be much record of notice of it taken by the Popes. Still, there seems to be evidence enough that even in that troubled period the Popes were not ignorant of the Holy House, and that, as far as prudence then permitted, they showed their recognition of its sacred character.

If we could but be sure of the genuineness of the Recanati priors' letter already spoken of (which still has its defenders among men of note), nothing further would be needed to prove that the information, both as to the arrival of the Holy House at Loreto and its changes of position there, had been at once communicated to the reigning Pontiff, Boniface VIII. It would seem, indeed, that this must have of necessity been done, whatever be thought with reference to the letter.

But, to confine ourselves to indisputable records, we have seen already how within fifty years of the time of its arrival, for the benefit of those unable to go to Loreto, the Avignon Pope Benedict XII granted indulgences in 1341 to those who at Recanati visited a picture of Our Lady of Loreto in the church of St. Gabriel; and from this it seems safe to conclude that other Indulgences had been then already granted to those visiting the Holy House itself.

We have seen, too, how another of the Avignon Popes, Blessed Urban V, had sought in 1367 to console the people of Tersatto, still grieving over their loss, by sending them a picture of Our Lady by St. Luke. Facts like these prove sufficiently that, even in their exile at Avignon, the Popes were well informed about the Holy House and its translations. Nor did even the troubles of the Schism, says Riera, deter Pope Urban VI from granting indulgences by word of mouth, if not in letters, to those visiting the Holy House upon the Feast of Our Lady's Nativity.[128]

The election of Martin V brought the Schism to an end in 1417, and proved the opening of a new era for the Holy House.

---

[128] Martorelli, *Teatro Istorico della Santa Casa*, vol. 1, 47.

"This glorious Pope," says Riera, "turned his thoughts to the exaltation of this most sacred House, and by Letters Patent Apostolic granted many privileges, indults, and immunities to those going thither."[129]

Without attempting to enumerate the favors granted by the Pontiffs to Loreto, it will suffice to lay before the reader a few of their more important utterances, selecting those especially that affirm the identity of the building now venerated there with the former habitation of the Holy Family at Nazareth.

According to the invariable usage of the Holy See in such matters, the Popes in their earlier grants expressed themselves in very guarded language, grounding their concessions on the devotion of the pilgrims, without mention of the Holy House as such. As fresh evidences came to light, however, revealing more and more the real nature of the little building, we find their language growing more explicit, until at last, after repeated investigations, the whole story of the miraculous translation is affirmed by them without any qualifying phrases.

The first apparently to make a pronouncement of this kind was Pope Paul II, whose miraculous cure has been related, and who, as we have seen, in his bull of 1470, proclaimed the "miraculous founding, or setting down, outside of Recanati, of the church of the Blessed Mary of Loreto with our Blessed Lady's image, by the ministry of Angels." The church here spoken of was, of course, the Holy House itself; but Pope Paul II thought it sufficient to speak of its miraculous appearance at Loreto, without declaring its identity with the House of Nazareth.

A little later we find Julius II going a step further. This Pope, in his devotion to the Holy House, made Loreto an immediate

[129] Ibid., 45.

dependency of the Holy See, and in the bull issued for that purpose on October 21, 1507, he states without any ambiguity, as his reason for so doing, the fact that the church of Loreto, according to pious belief and tradition, contained not only the actual image (or likeness) of the Blessed Virgin Mary but the very room or chamber in which she was herself conceived and brought up, and in which, when saluted by the angel, she conceived the Savior of all ages, and nourished ... and brought up her firstborn Son.

After speaking of the Holy House as having been consecrated by the Apostles as the first church dedicated to God's honor and that of the Blessed Virgin, and the first in which Mass was celebrated (which must be understood, says Father Hutchison, as meaning the first place after the *Coenaculum*), the Pope goes on to tell how the Holy House had been "carried by the hands of Angels from Nazareth into the country of Slavonia to the place called Fiume"; and from thence in the same way "to the wood of Laureta, a lady particularly devout to the Blessed Virgin"; and then, in consequence of the crimes there committed, to the hill of the two brothers, whence it had been finally translated ... to the high road of the Recanati territory."[130]

Here we have the whole story of the translation of the Holy House told in an authoritative papal document. Some critics have tried, however, to deprive its testimony of its force by laying stress upon the qualifying phrases — "*ut pie creditur et fama est*," with which the Pontiff introduces it. Father Eschbach shows, however, that the use of such phrases was, according to

---

[130] The above is taken from Julius II's bull of 1507, as quoted by Paul III, February 18, 1536. See Chevalier, *Notre-Dame de Lorette*, 334.

the custom of the Holy See, purely precautionary and did not imply uncertainty or doubt. In any case, we shall see the same story told in later pronouncements of the Popes without any such precautionary limitations. Through the mistake, made evidently by some scribe, in the Vatican and Loreto manuscripts of Julius II's bull, Bethlehem is named, instead of Nazareth, as the place from which the Holy House had come, though it is spoken of in the same document as the scene of the Annunciation. In spite of the absurdity of supposing the Pope to have thought that the Annunciation had taken place at Bethlehem, M. Chevalier professes to see in this "an error of enormous import"; and he actually goes on to argue from it that "in Rome, in the beginning of the sixteenth century, the legend was still but floating and uncertain."[131]

We have seen already how Leo X, who succeeded Julius II, repeated the same story in his brief of 1519, after receiving the Schedula brought by the Illyrians from the archives of Tersatto, and in like manner we find Pius IV, in a brief of October 9, 1565, describe the Holy House as: "That lowly and most sacred little cell, in which the Queen of Heaven was conceived, born, brought up, and hailed Mother of God by the Angel Gabriel, and which, with her image, has been translated by Angelic ministry from the city of Nazareth into the country of Picenum, as is proved by the testimony of persons worthy of belief."[132]

From this time, indeed, the Pontiffs seem to have seized every opportunity of proclaiming their belief in the identity of the Loreto House with that originally at Nazareth. Thus St. Pius V (1566–1572) caused *Agnus Deis* to be made, on which was

---

[131] Ibid., 71, 268.
[132] Ibid., 350.

stamped a representation of the Holy House, bearing the following inscription: *Vere Domus florida, qua fuit in Nazareth;*[133] and his successor Gregory XIII (1572–1585) had pieces of money coined and stamped with the same impression.[134]

Even more significant was the act of Pope Sixtus V, by which Loreto was made into a bishopric in 1586. For in the bull issued by him for that purpose, he states expressly that his reason for so doing was the fact that

> in the middle of its one illustrious collegiate church, there is that sacred Chamber consecrated by Divine mysteries, in which was born the Virgin Mary, and within which, being saluted by the Angel, she conceived of the Holy Ghost the Savior of the world, translated thither by the ministry of Angels; to which church, in consequence of the miracles which the Almighty through the intercession and merits of the Blessed Virgin Mary daily deigns to work within that Chamber, the faithful flock from all parts of the world for the sake of devotion and of making pilgrimage.[135]

In this bull, it will be noticed, all qualifying phrases disappear, the truth as to the Holy House having by this time been too solidly established to leave any need of their insertion.

---

[133] "The name *Agnus Dei* has been given to certain discs of wax impressed with the figure of a lamb and blessed at stated seasons by the Pope." Herbert Thurston, "Agnus Dei," *Catholic Encyclopedia*, vol. 1 (New York: Robert Appleton Company, 1907), http://www.newadvent.org/cathen/01220a.htm. —Ed.

[134] Eschbach, *La Vérité Sur le Fait de Lorette*, 319.

[135] Ibid., 320.

The House of the Virgin Mary

The same absence of any such phrases is also to be noticed in the inscription placed by the same Sixtus V on the facade of the basilica: *Deiparae Domus in qua Verbum caro factum est*; as also in the longer inscription, placed for the instruction of pilgrims by order of Clement VIII in 1595, on the east wall of the Holy House, in which is briefly told the history of its translations in terms of simple affirmation.

In 1670, Pope Clement X, by the advice of the Congregation of Rites, ordered the insertion of the following in the Roman Martyrology on December 10: *Laureti iii Piceno, Translatio sacrae Domus Dei Genetricis Mariae, in qua Verbum caro factum est*. This commemoration of the miraculous translation of the Holy House has since then been read each year, on the anniversary of its occurrence, in all cathedrals and collegiate churches in which the Divine Office is recited.

Before the end of the same century there followed, in 1699, under Pope Innocent XII, the approval by the Congregation of *Rites of Proper Lessons for the Feast of the Translation* to be recited in all the dioceses of the Province of Piceno. These *Lessons* contain a brief narration of the several translations of the Holy House, with a distinct assertion that it is "the very same in which the Word was made flesh and dwelt amongst us," and what makes this the more significant is the fact (which M. Chevalier himself relates) that in the debate that had preceded the issuing of the decree, the Promotor Fidei had laid before the Congregation reasons for modifying the positive assertions of the *Lessons* by inserting words to the effect that "it was an old and constant tradition proved by the testimony of many persons worthy of belief." At the same time, the Promotor Fidei himself, in making this proposal, had declared that "there could be no doubt as to the truth of what was told in the *Lessons*, both as to the miraculous translation of the

Holy House and as to its identity with the one in which the Angel had saluted Our Lady."[136] This plainly shows that in documents of this kind, even when such qualifying phrases are inserted, they must not be taken as expressing any real uncertainty. In this case, however, the suggestion of the Promotor was not accepted by the Congregation, and, without any such qualification, the *Lessons* were approved and ordered by the Pontiff to be used throughout the Province of Piceno.

The observance of the feast of the Translation of the Holy House, with the abovementioned *Proper Lessons*, was extended later to many other dioceses of different countries, including that of Rome itself.

The above quotations are more than enough to show how unreservedly the belief in the translation of the Holy House from Nazareth to Loreto has received the approbation of the Holy See; an approbation that has been again and again confirmed by later Pontiffs.

Thus, in an apostolic letter, dated August 22, 1846, soon after his accession, we find Pius IX exclaiming:

> Is it not by an unparalleled miracle that this Holy House was brought over land and sea from Galilee into Italy? By a supreme act of benevolence on the part of the God of all mercy, it has been placed in our pontifical domain, where for so many centuries it has become the object of the veneration of all the nations of the world and is resplendent with incessant miracles.

Again, in a bull of August 26, 1852, Pope Pius IX, in granting fresh privileges to the Holy House, says:

[136] Chevalier, *Notre-Dame de Lorette*, 408.

The House of the Virgin Mary

It is in reality the House of Nazareth that is venerated at Loreto, that House dear to God by so many claims, built originally in Galilee, separated from its foundations, and carried by Divine power across the seas into Dalmatia first, and thence into Italy—the blessed House where the most Holy Virgin, predestined from all eternity and perfectly exempt from original sin, was conceived, was born, was brought up; where Heaven's messenger saluted her as full of grace; where ... she became the Mother of the only Son of God.[137]

Pope Leo XIII, on occasion of the sixth centenary of the translation of the Holy House in 1895, did not hesitate to issue an encyclical letter calling on all the faithful, and especially on those of Italy, to join in its celebration and granting a Jubilee indulgence to those who visited the Holy House within the time prescribed. "We gladly embrace this occasion," he said in this encyclical,

to stir up the devotion of all the faithful toward the earthly Home of the Holy Family, and the mysteries wrought within its walls.... In that most blessed House took place the beginnings of man's salvation by the great and admirable Mystery of God made man.... Amid the poverty of this retired dwelling there lived those models of domestic life and harmony, a spectacle to Angels, to which we ourselves have more than once endeavored to recall and conform all families.

It is truly painful to read M. Chevalier's disrespectful comment on this apostolic letter of Pope Leo. "Would to God," he

---

[137] Ibid., 66.

presumptuously writes, "that from an historic point of view the ground on which this encyclical rests were as firm as its literary beauty is exalted!"[138] If individuals may thus sit in judgment on the utterances of Christ's Vicar, what, we may ask, is to become of his authority?

As to our late Holy Father Pope Pius X, his displeasure at the informal permission obtained by M. Chevalier for the publication of his work has been already mentioned, as shown by a published letter of Cardinal Merry del Val, written by His Holiness's order;[139] and, indeed, it is difficult to believe that, in writing his encyclical *Pascendi Gregis* in the year following the appearance of M. Chevalier's *Notre-Dame de Lorette*, the Pontiff had not in his mind that very book, when he made it one of the duties of the Councils of Vigilance created by him, "not to neglect books treating of the pious traditions of different places."

On hearing also of the formation of a college of writers in defense of the Holy House, the cardinal secretary of state wrote, on December 1 of the same year (1907), to say how pleased the Holy Father was that "the most worthy and opportune end of this association should be the promotion of devotion to the Holy House, and the protecting of it against insidious modern criticism."[140]

That the belief of Pope Pius X with reference to Loreto was identical with that of the Popes who have preceded him was shown by the words in which he answered the request of Msgr. Emidio Trenta to be allowed to receive episcopal consecration in the Holy House itself. In granting this request the Pontiff

---

[138] Chevalier, *Notre-Dame de Lorette*, 462.
[139] See p. 7, note 7 of this book.
[140] *L'abbé J. Faurax*, vol. iv, 33.

prayed that, "together with the fullness of the priesthood, he might receive every grace from God in that very sanctuary *in quo Verbum caro factum est.*"[141]

Finally, the esteem in which the Holy House is held by our present Holy Father Pope Benedict XV may be judged from the solicitude with which he has endeavored, during the war now raging,[142] to secure the immunity of the Sanctuary of Loreto from attack; describing it (if he has been reported rightly) as "the gem of the whole earth." As showing what should be the attitude of loyal Catholics with reference to the above pronouncements of the Popes, *we* cannot do better than quote from the *Tablet* of September 26, 1914, the following letter of his lordship the Bishop of Victoria, British Columbia, author of a valuable work in defense of the Holy House:

Sir,

Your reviewer (p. 244, August 15) deems it "very doubt-ful" whether the Holy See will ever decide the question of the authenticity of the Holy House of Loreto. The fact is, that the question has long been a *res judicata*. In pontifical document after pontifical document it has been categorically affirmed that the Holy House of Loreto is the Virgin's earthly home, borne away from Nazareth by the ministry of Angels. The matter is one in which the Holy See is the court of last resort: (1) because there is question of the authenticity of a sacred relic; and (2) because there is question of a miracle. I do not say that the decision of the Holy See in such questions is irreformable, but I do say

---

[141] *Bibliographie Loretaine* (1913), 137.
[142] World War I. —Ed.

that it is authoritative. Of course, it is open to a Catholic writer to pick flaws in it, if he can. But in that case, he should submit his thesis to the Holy See before publishing it to the world — else he is rightly held guilty of contempt of the highest ecclesiastical court in Christendom.
Yours etc.

+ALEXANDER MACDONALD
VICTORIA, B.C.
August 31, 1914

In this same connection we may also remind the reader of the passage, quoted in our first chapter, from Dr. Northcote's *Celebrated Shrines of the Madonna*.

Chapter 13

Saints' Devotion to Loreto

Next to the authoritative approbation given to Loreto by the Popes, probably nothing has done more to confirm the faithful's belief in it than the saints' intense devotion to it.

A list of more than sixty saints, canonized or beatified, who had made the pilgrimage to Loreto, was published by Bishop Martorelli in his work on the Holy House in 1733, and other saints of a later date could now, of course, be added. But what is most remarkable with reference to these sainted pilgrims is not so much their number as the rapturous devotion with which the Holy House inspired them, and the special favors received by many of them within its sacred walls. Not but that, in a less degree, similar effects have also been experienced by members of the simple faithful, who in fitting dispositions have approached the Sanctuary; but that this should have been especially the case with reference to those of God's servants who were the most enlightened and the least liable to illusion may surely be regarded as an additional proof of the exceptional sanctity of the Loreto shrine.

The following few instances, gathered from Martorelli and from other sources, will serve as a sufficient illustration.

The House of the Virgin Mary

Two visits to Loreto of St. Francis Xavier are recorded by Father Renzoli, in his *Santa Casa illustrata e difesa*,[143] which says that the saint went there "to pay his respects to Our Lady in her own House." The first of these was made in company with St. Ignatius and his other first disciples, when they were on their way to Rome to obtain from the Pope the confirmation of their order. The second was not long before his setting out for the far-distant Indies, of which he was to become the apostle, and on this occasion, as he himself acknowledged, when he was offering up the holy sacrifice in the Holy House, and with the miraculous image of Our Lady facing him, the Blessed Virgin breathed into his soul that wondrous zeal and courage that made India and even the whole world seem to him but little if they could only be gained for God.

We have seen already how Pope Pius II, on setting out from Rome to Loreto, felt the malady that was afflicting him diminish the nearer he drew to the Holy House. The same is told of St. Francis Borgia, who made three pilgrimages to Loreto. On one of these occasions he had set out tormented with a fever, which he found grew less and less as he approached the Holy House, and which on his reaching it left him altogether. His last pilgrimage was made when the hand of death was already on him, and when, in spite of grievous sufferings, he went to Loreto to ask Our Lady's final blessing on himself and on the order of which he was the general; and this order Our Blessed Lady in a vision showed him gathered underneath her mantle.

The great St. Charles Borromeo is declared in the process of his canonization to have been "a frequent visitor to the Holy House." His last visit to it was paid in 1579, when he celebrated

[143] Martorelli, *Teatro Istorico della Santa Casa*, vol. 2, 340.

there with extraordinary devotion the feast of the Nativity of Our Lady, after traveling for fifty miles on foot, praying and meditating all the way. He reached Loreto on the vigil of the feast and spent the whole night praying in the Holy House; after which, without going out of the Basilica, he sang Pontifical High Mass and preached with such fervor on the love of Our Blessed Lord, "who within that little chamber had taken flesh for our salvation and there had lived for years in obscurity and poverty," that his whole audience, of whom a great number received Communion from him, was moved to tears.

St. Aloysius Gonzaga—both to fulfill a vow, made by his mother at his birth (when his life as well as hers had been in danger) and to satisfy his own devotion—visited Loreto on his way to Rome, where he was about to enter the Society of Jesus. There he received Holy Communion on the morning of his arrival, and again on the following day. "He could scarcely," says Father Meschler,

> tear himself away from the Holy House, and spent hours full of sweetest consolation, praying in the sacred rooms where our Savior and His Blessed Mother had once lived ... and could not cease thanking God for the priceless graces that He had here granted to the human race.[144]

As another instance of a miraculous cure wrought at Loreto on a saint, we may mention what is told of St. James of La Marca, of the order of St. Francis, who died in 1476. Finding himself hindered in his work of preaching by a complication of diseases that were fast wearing his life away, this saint had recourse to

---

[144] Maurice Meschler, *Life of St. Aloysius Gonzaga, Patron of Christian Youth* (London: B. Herder, 1911), 118.

Our Lady of Loreto; and, as he was saying Mass there in the Holy House, the Blessed Virgin appeared to him after the Consecration and bade him ask for some other favor, as his health already was restored to him, and at that very instant he perceived it was.

St. Stanislaus Kostka, while praying in the Holy House, felt himself inflamed with such burning feelings of devotion, that afterward even in the severest winter weather he often was obliged to cool the intense heat of his heart with freezing water. St. Francis of Sales, says Father Hutchison,

> went on foot from Rome to Loreto, and no sooner had he entered the Holy House than, his biographer tells us, he was surprised by a flood of devout affections, and frequently kissed the walls which had been consecrated by the presence of Jesus, Mary, and Joseph. He confessed and communicated there, and then dissolving in loving sighs, he began to cry out, "These then are thy tabernacles, O beautiful Spouse of the eternal King! Here then, O Divine Lover, thou wast accustomed to remain looking through the lattices! Here Thou didst feed amidst lilies! Here Thou didst become my Brother! Oh, who will grant me to find Thee without, nestling in the breast of Thy Mother?... O God, who art the Master of Truth, from my most tender age Thou hast ever instructed me, and in this place I hope that Thou wilt enlighten me the more fully!" He then renewed the vow of virginity, which he had previously made in Paris.[145]

A second visit to Loreto was paid by St. Francis of Sales on occasion of his appointment as coadjutor bishop of Geneva.

---

[145] Hutchison, *Loreto and Nazareth*, 52.

Another saint especially remarkable for his devotion to Loreto was St. Benedict Joseph Labre. "Indeed," says Father Hutchison,

> his journeys to the Holy House were so frequent, and his behavior there was so edifying, that he was called the Saint of Loreto.... From the first time of visiting it he was so affected that he could not satiate himself with seeing it, venerating it, melting into tears, and with loving affection kissing again and again those holy walls, and inflaming his heart more strongly with love for the Holy Mother of God. In his last journey he himself prophesied that it would be the last of his life.[146]

And it was so proved by the event.

A like warning of his approaching end was given to another saintly pilgrim to the Holy House, St. Francis Caracciolo, of whom we read in the Breviary that "while he was persevering in prayer, in the sacred church of Loreto, it was made known to him that the end of his life was near."

No saint, however, has probably exceeded in his lifelong devotion to the Holy House the Blessed Anthony Grassi, the Oratorian of the neighboring city of Fermo, who in our own days has been raised to the altars. "Fermo," says his biographer,

> was the chief city of the delegate of the Marches, in which Loreto stood; and this local prerogative, combined with the early example imbibed from his father, gave Blessed Anthony a very special devotion to the Holy House of Loreto, to which he made many visits both before and after he entered the Oratory....

[146] Ibid., 53.

The House of the Virgin Mary

"O happy are we of Fermo," he used to exclaim, "who dwell near that spot where Divine grace inundated the Holy House, and made Mary a sea of all good things for us!" Fermo, he used to plead—being favored by God as the chief city of the province in which the Holy House had descended—its citizens ought to adorn their city with their virtues and mutual charity.

In 1621, when on a pilgrimage to Loreto, Blessed Anthony —then not many years a priest—was struck by lightning while kneeling in the church, on the steps at the west end of the Holy House. He was carried out in apparently a dying state, and traces of scorching were found afterward upon his underclothing, although he so rapidly recovered as to be able to return to Fermo the next day. "Our Holy Mother," he said in his own written account of it, "not only saved me from death, but gave me back my health in a better state than it had been previous to this accident. Before that time I used to suffer acute pain from indigestion, but ever since, I have been free from this." In thanksgiving for his preservation Blessed Anthony made two resolutions, which he faithfully adhered to throughout his long life: to make an act of thanksgiving each day and to make a pilgrimage to Loreto each year.

He loved to call the Holy House the House of the Annunciation; and on entering it, the first thing he always did was to throw himself on his knees and repeat the first chapter of St. John. His soul became absorbed in the mysteries of God from the moment he found himself within the sacred walls, and he was known to remain there for six hours at prayer without a word passing his lips.

His last pilgrimage was made in the last year of his life, in 1671, when he was about to enter on his eightieth year. He had knelt for hours quite rapt in prayer, when his companion, who had been loath to interrupt him sooner, touched him on the shoulder and told him it was time to go. "Let me stay a little longer," he pleaded, "for this is the last time that I shall visit this sanctuary. I must take my leave of the most Holy Virgin." At length his companion was constrained to lead the feeble old man away with gentle force. As he left the Holy House the servant of God broke into sobs and, turning around once more, said, "To thee, O Mary, do I commend my last end." The House of the Annunciation, his biographer remarks, "was the only place on this earth which it cost the Blessed Anthony any pang to leave."[147]

Another example may be taken from the autobiography of a servant of God of our own time, Sister Thérèse of Lisieux, known as the Little Flower of Jesus. In the wonderfully touching account of God's dealings with her soul, written at the command of her superior, and with no thought that it ever would be published, the Little Flower thus speaks of the visit to Loreto paid by her in 1887 in company with her father and her sister:

What shall I say of the Holy House? I was overwhelmed with emotion when I realized that I was under the very roof that had sheltered the Holy Family, gazed on the same walls our Lord had looked on, trod the ground once moistened with the sweat of St. Joseph's toil, and saw the little chamber of the Annunciation, where the Blessed Virgin Mary held Jesus in her arms after she had borne Him there in her virginal womb, even put my rosary into the little porringer used by the Divine Child.

[147] Amabel Kerr and Antonio Grassi, *A Saint of the Oratory, the Life of Blessed Antony Grassi* (London: Burns and Oates, 1901), 33–38, 189, 190.

How sweet these memories! But our greatest joy was to receive Jesus in His own House, and thus become His living temple in the very place which He had honored by His Divine Presence.... My father with his habitual gentleness followed the other pilgrims to the Altar of the Blessed Sacrament, where Holy Communion is ordinarily given; but his daughters, less easily satisfied, went toward the Holy House. God favored us, for a priest was on the point of celebrating Mass. We told him of our great wish, and he immediately asked for two hosts, which he placed on the paten. You may picture, dear mother, the ecstatic happiness of that Communion; no words can describe it. What will be our joy when we communicate eternally in the dwelling of the King of Heaven![148]

Before leaving this subject, it would not do to omit to mention three other great servants of God, no less famous for their learning than their sanctity, who have borne testimony to their belief in the Holy House, not only by their pilgrimages to it, but also in their writings: Blessed Peter Canisius, one of St. Ignatius's first disciples; the venerable Cardinal Baronius, the Father of Church History; and St. Alphonsus Liguori, who has been declared a Doctor of the Church.

The first of these, Blessed Peter Canisius, has been already spoken of in connection with his praise of the Loreto historian Angelita. In his time an impious book called *De Idolo Lauretano* had been brought out by Vergerius, the apostate bishop of Capo

---

[148] Thérèse and Thomas Nimmo Taylor, *Soeur Thérèse of Lisieux, the Little Flower of Jesus; a New and Complete Translation of L'histoire D'une Âme, with an Account of Some Favours Attributed to the Intercession of Soeur Thérèse* (New York: Kennedy, 1912), 94.

d'Istria, who had joined the Lutherans. The very title of this blasphemous work reveals its nature, and to the refutation of it and similar attacks of the so-called Reformers, Blessed Canisius devoted an entire chapter of his great work *De Maria Deipara Virgine*, the first edition of which appeared in 1577. At Loreto, he says,

> there is to be seen the dwelling-place of Mary, or to use a more familiar term, her chamber, still consisting as of old of four walls composed of cement and stone, an ancient monument in truth to be as much admired as it is to be venerated. Having been first translated from Palestine into Dalmatia, it remained awhile near to the town of Fiume, and from thence was carried into Italy, where it continues in the possession of the people of Loreto.[149]

To the scoffs and ridicule heaped upon the story by Vergerius, Canisius then opposes the sober narratives of trustworthy historians, the constant and universal tradition of the inhabitants, which has been sanctioned by the Roman Pontiffs, and confirmed by continual miracles, conversions, and extraordinary graces bestowed on the pilgrims to Loreto, who flock to it from every quarter of the earth. "Has anyone," he asks, "ever visited Loreto (at all events if led by any motive of Christian piety) who has not seen with his own eyes and heard with his own ears the mighty works of God, and felt them in his soul?"[150]

Cardinal Baronius did not live long enough to deal in his *Annales* with the year 1291, in which took place the removal of the Holy House from Nazareth. Nevertheless in speaking in the

---

[149] Peter Canisius, *De Maria Deipara Virgine* (1577).

[150] Peter Canisius, "De Verbi Dei Corruptelis," bk. 2; "De Sacrosancta Virgine Maria Deipara" (1584), 585, 588.

first volume, which appeared in 1588, of the residence of the Holy Family at Nazareth, he took occasion to remark:

> That House, in which the most Holy Virgin received from heaven the intimation of the Incarnation of the Word, remains by a great miracle, not only still entire, but, having been rescued by the ministry of the Angels from the hands of the infidels, it was translated first into Dalmatia, and thence into Italy, into the territory of Loreto in the Province of Piceno. . . . Nor is there reason for anyone to doubt as to the fact, if he but remembers that in that House the Angel said that with God no word is impossible"; and that Christ foretold, as an article of the Christian faith, that at the bidding of Christians even mountains should be moved from place to place.[151]

With what devotion Baronius himself had made the pilgrimage to Loreto may be gathered from his own brief account of it in a letter to his father, dated May 2, 1568. "By God's grace, I said Mass at the most sacred altar in the Chapel itself of Our Lady of Loreto; and I remained alone in the very chapel in which is the Madonna (in the Santo Camino) as long as I wished, a favor granted only to a few."[152] Later on, as cardinal, Baronius spent two days at Loreto in 1598, in attendance on Pope Clement VIII, by whom a few years previously the inscription already spoken of, at the east end of the Holy House, had been erected, giving the history of its translations.

That the continuators of Baronius's *Annales* were of exactly the same mind as he is shown by their mentions of the translation of the Holy House in connection with the years 1291 and 1294.

---

[151] Cardinal Baronius, *Annales* (1588).
[152] "Vita del Card. Baronio per Generoso Calenzio," 120, 504.

St. Alphonsus Liguori made a pilgrimage to Loreto in 1772, when, having been obliged by the Pope to accept the bishopric of St. Agatha, he was waiting in Rome to receive consecration. His companion would have dissuaded him on account of the fatigue of such a journey, but Alphonsus replied: "Our good Mother will assist me. When shall I have such an opportunity again? Nothing will seem too much to weigh against the consolation of visiting the house in which the Eternal Word became man for me!" The three days spent by him at Loreto, says his biographer,

> were for him three days of unspeakable consolation. It might be said of him that he took up his dwelling in the Holy House. He noted, or rather meditated on, the most trifling local details, and was heard frequently to repeat tenderly: "So it was here that the Word of God was made man! Here that Mary held Him in her arms!" One morning he asked his companion to leave him alone for a time. When alone, he went into that innermost part of the Holy House which is behind the altar" [the Santo Camino, where Our Lady is believed to have been at the time of the Annunciation], and there we can easily imagine how deeply he must have contemplated that great mystery of the Incarnation.... The hour at last came when they must quit the celebrated shrine, but Alphonsus left his heart there when he departed. On his return he could speak of nothing but the great mystery which had been accomplished there.[153]

[153] Augustin Berthe and Harold Castle, *Life of St. Alphonsus de Liguori, Bishop and Doctor of the Church, Founder of the Congregation of the Most Holy Redeemer*, vol. 2 (Dublin: James Duffy, 1905), 14–15.

In confutation of a disedifying book, written by a priest named Rolli, in which the miraculous translation of the Holy House was spoken of as a fable, and the titles given to Our Lady in the Litany of Loreto were irreverently criticized, St. Alphonsus, in 1775, wrote a brief reply, which in some editions of his *Glories of Mary* may be found as an appendix. In this, the holy Doctor points out that the irreverent critic is but "following in the track of Launay, Vergerius, Hospinien, and other Protestants, who have been refuted with unanswerable evidence"; and he quotes Pope Benedict XIV as declaring the authenticity of the translation to be "proved as well by ancient monuments and unbroken tradition, as by the testimony of Sovereign Pontiffs, the common consent of the faithful, and the continual miracles which are there worked even to the present day."[154]

A well-known Belgian Redemptorist priest and writer expressed himself on this subject as follows in a letter to the present writer: "We [believers in Loreto] are in such good society, such a noble army! We are with *all the Saints, all the Popes*, all the truly learned and humble writers!" What has been told above suffices surely to show the truth of the good Father's remark.

We may conclude this chapter by relating the incident of which Father Riera was himself an eyewitness in 1559, with reference to the pilgrimages from Tersatto to Loreto. There could hardly be a stronger confirmation of the miraculous translation of the Holy House than this. "I was sitting," Father Riera writes,

> in the church at Loreto hearing confessions, when I heard a most unusual disturbance and the sound of much crying

---

[154] Alfonso Maria de Liguori, "A Short Reply to the Extravagant Reform Attempted by the Abbé Rolli," in *The Glories of Mary*, ed. Bishop Coffin (1868).

and groaning. I came out of the confessional to enquire into its cause, and there at the threshold of the church saw kneeling from four to five hundred Dalmatians, men, women, and children, divided into different companies, each company under the direction of a priest, and all crying out with sighs and tears, "Return, return to us, O Mary! O most holy Mary, return to Fiume!" Touched with compassion for their distress, I drew near to a venerable priest who was amongst them, and asked the cause of their sorrow; with a deep sigh, he answered: "Ah! they have only too much cause"; and again he repeated with still greater energy, "Return, return to us, O Mary!" When they advanced within the church, and arrived where they could see the entrance to the Holy House, their cries and their sobs grew yet louder. I tried as well as I could to as-suage their grief, and to direct them to look for consola-tion from heaven; but the old man interrupted me and said: "Suffer them to weep, Father; their lamentations are only too reasonable; that which you now possess was once ours." At last I was obliged to exert my authority to restore order and enforce silence, and indeed, their prayers were so earnest that I could not but fear that God would listen to their request.

The same thing, in a greater or less degree, happened, says Riera, each year that he spent at Loreto; and Tor-sellini (forty years later) affirms the same with reference to his time. In fact, these pilgrimages of Dalmatians to Loreto are spoken of as still continuing as late as 1784.[155]

---

[155] Translated from Riera by Northcote, *Celebrated Sanctuaries*, 83.

The House of the Virgin Mary

That a whole people should thus have continued for centuries to travel to Loreto, to beseech Our Lady once more to bring her house to them, must be admitted to be wholly incapable of explanation, unless upon the supposition that (as the historians both of Tersatto and Loreto tell us) the Holy House had first rested for a time on the hill above Fiume.

Chapter 14

Some Objections Answered

The chief objections brought by the opponents of the tradition have been directly or indirectly dealt with in the course of our narrative. It has, however, been a disappointment to find in the recently completed *Catholic Encyclopedia*, in its article on the Santa Casa, a very halfhearted defense of it, with concessions to its modern critics that seem quite uncalled for. Considering, therefore, the high character and great influence of the work in which the article appears, it seems necessary to add some remarks upon it.

With the first part of the article we have indeed no quarrel; its writer — Father H. Thurston, S.J. — mentions without dispute the sanction given to the Loreto tradition by the Popes, the saints' devotion to it, the miracles by which it is said to have been confirmed, the absence of foundations to the Holy House, and so forth.

Very different, however, is the tone of the concluding portion of the article, and quite at variance with what has, I think, been proved in the foregoing chapters. "Recent historical criticism has shown," says Father Thurston, "that in other directions the Lauretan tradition is beset with difficulties of the gravest kind," as "presented in the work of Canon Chevalier ... the substance of whose argument has yet found no adequate reply."

It would, I think, be difficult for anyone to speak thus, who side by side with Chevalier's work had read the sober, scholarly reply of Father Eschbach, so often quoted in these pages. The success of M. Chevalier's book has been largely due to the learning displayed in it as a piece of bibliography, hardly any writer on Nazareth or Loreto being left unmentioned in it, whether relevantly or not to the real point at issue. M. Chevalier's general contention is summarized by Father Thurston under headings that, at the risk of some repetition, will be best considered separately.

1. It is objected that, from the accounts of pilgrims who visited Nazareth before the date of the translation, no cottage was then venerated there "which could correspond in any satisfactory way with the present Santa Casa at Loreto"; and that what was pointed out to pilgrims as the abode of the Blessed Virgin "was a sort of natural cavern in the rock."

It is true that the brief and incomplete accounts of early visitors to Nazareth — presented as they are in M. Chevalier's pages in chronological order, and with equal prominence given to the many that tell us nothing, or at least nothing to our purpose, and to the few that tell us more — produce upon the reader a confusing and unsatisfactory effect. But to show that some of them do make mention of a building sufficiently corresponding to the Santa Casa, we need but remind the reader of the words of the monk Phocas, who declared that in the crypt "you have before you the actual former house of Joseph"; and of the assertion of John of Würzburg that in his day "the chamber of the Annunciation was still shown there." Least of all must we forget the words of the Dominican Ricoldo, who, a few years before the date of its translation, described it as "the only one of the original buildings still remaining ... preserved by God as a memorial of humility and poverty." From clear expressions such as these we see how to interpret the defective and obscure accounts of others.

Neither need we be disturbed to find many pilgrims speaking of the scene of the Annunciation as a cave, since it has never been disputed that the cave still shown at Nazareth was once a portion of the habitation of the Holy Family, the house having been built in front of the opening to it. Moreover the very pilgrims named above, as speaking of the Holy House, describe it as existing in their time in a crypt—itself a kind of cave or grotto—from which they passed into the house and the cave behind it.

It is not surprising, therefore, that they should have described the whole sanctuary as a cave. That in the time of these pilgrims it should have been found beneath the flooring of the church is explained as follows by Burchard of Mount Sion, who visited Nazareth about 1284. "Nearly all the places," says this pilgrim,

> in which anything was done by our Lord, are underground, and you go down to them by several steps into a crypt; as is *the place of the Annunciation*, and of the Nativity, and this at Cana in Galilee, and many others, which are shown below the ground. For this I can find no other reason than that on account of the repeated destruction of the churches, in which the actual places were, the ruins were piled up upon the ground; and when these had been leveled in some sort of fashion, other buildings were erected on them. But the Christians, whose devotion led them to visit these places, and get to the actual spots

where the events took place, were obliged to clear from them the debris, and to make steps by which they might be reached. Thus nearly all these places seem to be as it were in crypts.[156]

2. The next difficulty advanced by Father Thurston from Chevalier's book is based on the silence as to the events of the translation, on the part of both Oriental chronicles and pilgrims, for two centuries after the time assigned to it, "there being no word of the disappearance at Nazareth of a shrine formerly held in veneration there ... nor, until the sixteenth century, among Orientals any hint of a consciousness of their loss, and then the idea was suggested from the West."

With reference to the alleged silence of Oriental chronicles, it seems but reasonable to ask: What chronicles were there in Galilee at the time in question, in which a mention of the disappearance of the Holy House could be looked for? At the same time, that Eastern testimony to the fact of its previous preservation there is not altogether wanting is shown by the already quoted words of the Arab traveler of the twelfth century, Abul Hassan Aly, affirming the existence then of the House of Miriam at Nazareth.[157]

As to the pilgrims, it is certainly untrue to say that from them nothing is heard of its disappearance from Nazareth till two centuries later; since we have seen from Jerome of Raggiolo that, long before that time, the pilgrims all came back declaring its translation to Loreto. We saw, too, how the same thing was confirmed by the Landgrave of Hesse, as well as by the

---

[156] Laurent, *Peregrinatores Medii Aevi Quatuor*, 44.
[157] See p. 26, note 23 of this book.

very attempt of Suriano to combat the idea.[158] Nor ought it to be thought surprising that no mention of it should have been made by the few pilgrims who, during the first hundred years or so after the translation of the Holy House, made their way to Nazareth at the peril of their lives and at the cost of heavy bribes to the Saracens in possession of it. The envoys from Tersatto and Picenum, who were sent immediately after the translation, are said to have found some Christians still surviving, who showed them where the Holy House had stood. But the pilgrims who came a little later all speak of the place as inhabitated by none but the fiercest Saracens. The foundations doubtless were still visible; but with no one to explain things to them, their real significance would easily be lost upon the pious visitors; and so the pilgrims of that period speak naturally of nothing but of the cave that they saw remaining, with some mosaic decorations, and of a pillar that they supposed to mark the spot occupied by Our Lady when the Angel visited her. It may perhaps be true that later on people at Nazareth were made conscious of the loss they had sustained by reports brought to them from Loreto; but it is hard to see how this can be used as any argument against the translation.

3. A third objection is drawn from the existence of certain documents that are said to prove that the church of St. Mary of Loreto was in existence as early as the twelfth century; and that therefore it cannot have been translated thither in 1294, as asserted in the Loreto legend. The documents referred to are:

  1. A charter dated January 4, 1193(4), by which Bishop Jordan of the now extinct See of Humana, near Ancona,

[158] See chap. 10.

made over to the Camaldolese Monks of Fonte Avellano the parochial church "Sanctae Mariae quae exita in fundo Laureti."

2. An inventory of the lands attached to the bishopric of Recanati, drawn up in 1285, in which the same church of Our Lady of Loreto is named, as marking the position of certain of the Bishop's lands: "Item habet in fundo Laureti juxta ecclesiam Sanctae Mariae de Laureto et viam modiolos III, staria VII."

These documents were first brought into notice early in the last century by Vogel and Leopardi, and Canon Chevalier speaks of the difficulty suggested by them as overwhelming (*ecrasante*). It will be seen at once, however, that any difficulty they may present depends entirely on the supposed identity of the church of Our Lady, mentioned in them, with the little building venerated at Loreto as the Holy House. When, therefore, it is shown that, both in character and situation, they differed from each other altogether, the whole difficulty is seen to disappear.

If the name Loreto had always been used in its present restricted sense, as designating no more than the summit of the hill on which now stands the basilica, it would, of course, have been difficult to suppose within so limited an area the existence of two churches bearing the same title of St. Mary of Loreto. But many documents prove that in the Middle Ages its designation was much wider; and that in that part of Italy the name Lauretum (laurel grove) was used not at all uncommonly of estates on which laurels grew. Thus, a diploma of the emperor Conrad mentions, on the same coast near to Sinigaglia, "the estate of the greater and lesser Lauretum" ("*fundum Laureti majoris et minoris*"); and a bull of Alexander II names in the County of Ancona the church "S. Laurentii de Laureto;" as well as another "*in Laureto majori.*"[159]

In the territory of Recanati, the division, or estate, known as the Fundus Laureti (in which stood the church of Our Lady mentioned in the documents of 1193 and 1285) embraced, says Father Eschbach, much more than the hill of the basilica, and answered to the present Diocese of Loreto, containing about seventeen square kilometers. That the church in this Fundus Laureti, which was made over to the Camaldolese Monks in 1193(4), was quite different from the Holy House is clear from the description given of it. For it is called in the document a parochial church, which the poor little Santa Casa certainly never was; and is described as having attached to it vineyards, groves of olives and figs, watermills, and meadows, and other elements that can never have existed on the hill on which stands the Holy House, as will at once be understood by those knowing the locality. Moreover, it is spoken of in Bishop Jordan's charter as the church of St. Mary "*quae exita*[160] *in fundo Laureti.*" This Father Eschbach (following dictionaries of medieval Latin) translates as "at the exit, or extremity, of the Fundus Laureti." Now, on the plain stretching westward from Loreto hill, at a place precisely answering to the above description, at the point, namely, where the road issues from the old Fundus Laureti, and near to the river Musone, where watermills and meadows and similar properties are likely to have been, traces have been recently discovered of an ancient church, which from having had a cemetery attached to it is shown to have been a parish church. Of this, one of the

---

[159] Eschbach, *La Vérité Sur le Fait de Lorette*, 378–379.
[160] This, says Eschbach (*La Vérité Sur le Fait de Lorette*, 388), is the true reading; and not, as M. Chevalier gives it, "*quae est sita.*"

resident Penitentiary Fathers of Loreto assured the present writer in 1912.

Not far from the same spot there is now a church called S. Maria delle Brecce, which, according to the tradition of the locality, was built to replace one still more ancient, which was said to have existed before the coming of the Holy House and to have been destroyed in the Ghibelline wars.

There seems no room for doubting that the church, of which the remains have been thus discovered, was the "S. Maria in fundo Laureti" mentioned in the above-quoted ancient documents.

4. Father Thurston brings forward as his next objection M. Chevalier's assertion that "no writer can be shown to have heard of the miraculous translation of the Holy House before 1472, namely, 180 years after the event is supposed to have taken place."[161]

It has been shown, I think, abundantly in the preceding chapters that the Loreto tradition as to the miraculous translation, besides having been passed down from mouth to mouth through successive and continuous generations (which of itself would be sufficient evidence as to the truth of the fact), is based also on real historical and contemporary documents.

It is true that we no longer now possess the actual documents drawn up to attest it at the time itself; but though the documents themselves have perished, we know the full story they contained from writers whose reliability cannot be questioned, who studied them and made extracts from them while they were still in preservation.

---

[161] This year is assigned by Chevalier, in his *Notre-Dame de Lorette*, to Teramano's account of the translation. Later, however, he has given in to the earlier date of 1465.

Thus, at Tersatto—not to repeat what has been said as to the inscriptions and the pilgrimages to Loreto asking Our Lady to return—we saw that the original papers recording the arrival and departure of the Holy House, including the statement of the priest Alexander and his fellow envoys sent to Nazareth in 1291, had been safely preserved in the Convent Archives until as late as 1629. From these *Tersatto Papers* had been drawn up the Schedula (used by Angelita in his history in 1531), which the Illyrian envoys had brought to Recanati and which was forwarded to Pope Leo X. From these same papers also Father Glavinich (who himself tells us of the fire in which they were lost) had obtained the detailed account of the Holy House and its translations given by him in his *History of Tersatto*—which latter work, it must be remembered, M. Chevalier had been unable to consult.

At Recanati, in like manner, although the burning of the city archives in 1322 had involved the loss of the original document containing the depositions of the Sixteen Envoys sent to Nazareth in 1296, we saw that, as Riera tells us, officially signed copies of it had been nevertheless preserved in the chief families of the city. A summary of it is thus given us in Riera's history, and he makes special mention, among other copies, of the one received from the secretary of the commune by the ancestor of the Leopardi family. In 1565, in which Riera wrote, he had been assured, he says, by Dr. Bernardino Leopardi that he himself had often seen and read this copy. Canon Chevalier's only reply to this is to accuse this holy Jesuit of "having invented these details"![162]

Besides this, we ought not to forget what the same Father Riera tells, as to the account of the translation composed within

---

[162] Chevalier, *Notre-Dame de Lorette* 320, note.

fifty years of the event by Bishop Peter of Macerata (1328–1347), in whose diocese Recanati was then included. This account of it, says Riera, had been ordered to be used as a class book in the schools of Recanati; and in his own time ancient copies had been found, though apparently since lost.

We need not dwell again upon the Jesi will of 1348 providing help for pilgrims "to the Holy House of Mary"; nor upon the Jesi fresco of the same date,[163] clearly showing, as they do, how general already was the belief in the miraculous translation; for the facts already mentioned prove sufficiently how untrue it is to say that prior to the time of Teramano no mention of the translation can be found.

The writer feels justified, however, in returning for a moment to the subject of the Macerata document of 1315, containing the condemnation of the Ghibelline violators of Our Lady's "*Cona.*" The more he thinks about it, the more satisfied the writer feels that the word must there be taken as employed for *cuna*, meaning *home*, or *birthplace*, as explained already. It is well known how common is the use of *o* for *u*, both in medieval Latin and Italian; and none of the meanings given elsewhere to the word will at all suit the context. In this belief the concurrence of friends well qualified to judge has greatly strengthened him.[164] But if the judge of the Province of the Marches in 1315 is thus to be understood to have described, as Our Lady's *native home*, the little church

---

[163] See p. 79 of this book.

[164] It has been pointed out to the present writer by an expert scholar in Italian that the Neapolitan form of *cuna* is *connola*, and the Romagnol *conla*, the *o* in each case taking the place of *u*; and that thus, in the district of Loreto, *cona* may easily have been the current form of *cuna*.

that had been so mysteriously brought to Loreto only twenty-one years before, we have in this the clearest evidence that its history was then already generally known. It has been remarked already that, in the first revelations made both at Tersatto and Loreto, Our Lady is said to have declared the little church to have been the house in which she was born; and this is exactly what, whether in Latin or Italian, the word *cuna* would express.

As affording further proof of the early date at which news of the miraculous translation was spread abroad, we ought not to omit to mention some of the early fresco paintings in which it is found represented.

Of these, the one at Jesi, which has been already spoken of, is assigned by connoisseurs to the first half of the fourteenth century, while those at Gubbio and at Atri are said to belong to the middle and second half of the same — all of them, therefore, older by a hundred years, or more, than the earliest testimony to the translation allowed by M. Chevalier. It may be, indeed, that Father Thurston is correct in saying that "it is by no means safe to assume that every picture of Angels carrying a house must refer to Loreto." But in the case, at all events, of the Gubbio fresco (if the restoration of it may be trusted), no doubt can be any longer entertained as to the precise event depicted in it. In the upper portion of this fresco, our Blessed Lady is represented, surrounded by angels and directing the translation of the Holy House. On the left side, angels are seen lifting it up above the hill of Tersatto, on which is clearly depicted the lordly castle of the Frangipani, distinguished as it still is by its three towers — two round and one square. On the right side is shown the deposition of the Holy House in Loreto wood, while on the hill above is seen the narrow gate through which the traveler enters Recanati city from the Loreto road. The accuracy of these details seems to show, says Father Eschbach, that the painter had himself visited the places before setting to design the picture. The fresco is believed to be the work of Guido Palmarucci, who was living in Gubbio in 1349.[165]

5. Although Father Thurston admits that Pope Paul II, in 1464, declared "the church to have been miraculously founded," and the image of the Blessed Virgin "to have been brought there by Angels," he nevertheless objects that "all this differs widely from the details of later accounts."

It must be remembered that the above declaration of Pope Paul II is the first clear papal pronouncement on the subject, and it was, therefore, but to be expected that his words should be more restrained than those of his successors, who spoke after fuller investigations had been made. Thus, he contented himself with affirming what had been established by the testimony of abundantly sufficient witnesses — namely, the miraculous appearance of the little church with its image of Our Lady in a place where no such church had been before; although he remained still silent as to its identity with the house of Nazareth, in which he no doubt believed.

If we think it strange that the Pope should have spoken of the image without mentioning the Holy House, it is necessary, in order to understand his words aright, that we should bear in mind that, at the time referred to — the time, namely, of its appearance on the land of Recanati — the Holy House was not yet enclosed within any other building, but was itself (small though it was) the church or chapel of St. Mary that the Pope declared to have been miraculously founded or set down. When, therefore,

---

[165] Eschbach, *Lorette et l'Ultimatum de M. U. Chevalier*, 92–112.

he speaks of the church, he is actually speaking of the house, within which the image had been brought.

Thus, so far from being at variance with the statement made by Paul II, the later, more detailed accounts only filled in and completed the story.

As always happens in such cases, especially when authority has not yet spoken, some partly inaccurate accounts as to the origin of the Holy House, in which truth is mixed with error, appear to have been current at an early period. Thus, in the *Month* for July 1912, Father Thurston has told us of a fellow of Eton College, William Wey, who had picked up in Italy about the year 1458, among other notices of places of pilgrimage, the following description of Loreto: "There is there a chapel of Blessed Mary, which of old was built by St. Helen [*sic*] in the Holy Land," and "which was lifted up by the Angels and was carried away from the Holy Land to Alretum, while the country-folk and shepherds looked on." There is no evidence that Wey had himself visited Loreto; nor is it known whence he obtained this account of it; nor how long before his time it had been in circulation. However, the mistake made in it by its writer, in confusing the church built over the Holy House by St. Helen with the Holy House itself, does not destroy the value of its testimony to the miraculous translation. That for a time there should have been more or less various versions of the story current is only what was to be expected.

6. The next objection is based upon the "relative lateness" of the papal confirmations of the Loreto tradition; joined to the fact that these at first were introduced by the clause "*ut pie creditur et fama est,*" and "in obvious dependence on the extravagant leaflet compiled about 1472 by Teramano." We have remarked already that the authority of such papal pronouncements, whether they

be issued late or early, is the same; and enough has been said, in an earlier chapter, to show that the great difficulties of the time in question did more than suffice to explain in this case the comparative lateness of the papal confirmations of Loreto.

With reference, however, to the employment at first of precautionary phrases, such as "*ut pie creditor . . .*," one can indeed but wonder at its being brought up here as an objection; for it is well known that in cases of this kind such phrases are universally used by the Holy See, without any implication necessarily that the matter is looked upon as doubtful. We saw, moreover, that after a while all such precautionary phrases disappeared from the papal pronouncements on Loreto.

To those, also, who are acquainted with the facts, it will certainly seem strange to hear Teramano's summary described as an "extravagant leaflet"—as if it might be regarded as the mere fanciful production of some random scribbler. Far different, at all events, has been the judgment passed upon it by the Sovereign Pontiffs, by whose orders, translated into numerous languages, it has been set up on the walls of the basilica, for the instruction of the pilgrims, where for centuries it has continued to bear testimony to the miraculous translation of the Holy House.

It is true, of course, that the story of the translation told in papal documents is the same substantially as that of Teramano's summary. But if it be supposed (as seems to be implied in the objection) that Teramano's statements were blindly adopted by the Pontiffs without investigation of the facts, we can but look upon it as an unwarranted and unjustifiable suggestion, entirely at variance with the known practice of the Holy See.

Father Thurston concludes his article with the remark that "there is much to suggest that a sufficient explanation is afforded by the hypothesis that a miracle-working statue, or picture of the Madonna, was brought from Tersatto to Loreto by some pious Christians, and was then confounded with the ancient rustic chapel in which it was harbored, the veneration formerly given to the statue afterwards passing to the building."

It is not easy to deal seriously with a suggestion so entirely gratuitous, in support of which no evidence can be adduced, and which simply sets at nought the numberless proofs by which the miraculous translation is established. No one has ever heard of any such bringing of a statue or picture from Tersatto; and still less of the strangely foolish people who transferred their veneration from the statue to the building.

Though wonderful was the removal of the Holy House from Nazareth to Tersatto and Loreto, God, as Cardinal Newman says, could work this wonder; and if, as Catholics, we must admit that miracles do at times occur, it surely is both easier and more reasonable to believe in its miraculous translation than to suppose (as the above hypothesis requires) that the people both of Tersatto and Loreto, along with their most trusted writers, and innumerable famous saints, should have been so amazingly and deplorably deceived—to say nothing of the long line of cautious and sagacious Pontiffs, who, for century after century, have unceasingly affirmed it, including our present Holy Father Pope Benedict XV, the full text of whose authoritative declaration may be read in the appendix.

Appendix

Decree of the Sacred Congregation of Rites

The Sanctuary of Loreto more than all other shrines of Mary is rightly and deservedly regarded as illustrious, and to Christ's faithful it has been, for the last six centuries or so, the object of especial veneration and of highest honor, it being in fact the house in which the most Blessed Virgin Mary was born, and which divine mysteries have rendered sacred, since it was there that the Word was made flesh. That blessed house having been wonderfully translated long ago by the ministry of angels from the Holy Land of Palestine, first into Dalmatia, and thence into the territory of Loreto in the Province of Piceno, and having thus been deposited in the very bosom of the Catholic Church, stands preeminent as enriched with the power of continual miracles and of heavenly graces and benefits.

The feast of this wonderful translation, which toward the end of the seventeenth century was assigned to its proper day, namely, the tenth of December, has been without interruption duly celebrated each year in the churches of the said Province of Piceno and gradually also in those of other parts, both of Italy, and of very many other countries of the world, until the year 1913.[166]

---

[166] In 1914 the reformed calendar came into observance, in which, in addition to the universal feasts, only the local feasts of each diocese were retained.

The House of the Virgin Mary

Moved by all these facts, and well aware of the earnest desire of the flock entrusted to them, not to say of all faithful Catholics, the bishops of the dioceses of the Province of Piceno, in order to prevent the widespread devotion to so important a shrine of the Holy Virgin from becoming gradually impaired, have all earnestly besought our most Holy Lord Pope Benedict XV to restore the feast of the Translation of the Holy House of the Blessed Virgin Mary to its pristine honor, and to allow it to be annually celebrated.

Our most Holy Lord Pope Benedict XV, most graciously receiving this request, as laid before him by the undersigned Cardinal Pro-Prefect of the Sacred Congregation of Rites, and following also his own devotion to God's Mother, has decreed that the feast of the Translation of the Holy House of the Blessed Virgin Mary with the rite of a greater double shall be observed each year by each of the dioceses of Italy and the adjacent isles, as well as by the regular orders and religious families, even though using their own calendar, and dwelling within the limits of those dioceses, on the tenth day of December, with the proper Mass and Office already approved: the rubrics being observed.

Moreover, his same Holiness has graciously permitted that this feast of the Blessed Virgin Mary may also be extended, under the same terms and conditions, to all other dioceses and religious families, if the several most reverend ordinaries, or respective superiors, duly petition for it.

Anything to the contrary notwithstanding. The 12th day of April, 1916.

+Card. Ep. Portuen. et S. Rufinae, S.R.C., Pro-Praefectus
Alexander Verde, Secretarius

References

Acta Apostolicae Sedis. 1916.

Angelita, Girolamo. *De Almae Domus Lauretanae in Agro Recanatensi Mira Translatione Brevis, et Fidelis Enarratio.* 1531.

Baronius, Cardinal. *Annales.* 1588.

Bellasis, Edward. "Jottings About Cardinal Newman." *The Month* (October 1913).

Berthe, Augustin, and Harold Castle. *Life of St. Alphonsus de Liguori, Bishop and Doctor of the Church, Founder of the Congregation of the Most Holy Redeemer.* Vol. 2. Dublin: James Duffy, 1905.

Callistus, Nicephorus. *Ecclesiasticae Historiae.* Ca. 1320.

Canisius, Peter. *De Maria Deipara Virgine.* 1577.

———. *De Verbi Dei Corruptelis.* 1584.

Chevalier, Ulysse. *Notre-Dame de Lorette: Étude Historique Sur l'Authenticité de la Santa Casa.* Paris: A. Picard, 1906.

di Gesu, Rev. Alfonso. *Oppositori e Diffensori.*

Eschbach, Alphonse. *La Vérité Sur le Fait de Lorette: Exposé Historique et Critique*. Paris: Lethielleux, 1910.

———. *Lorette et l'Ultimatum de M. U. Chevalier*. 1915.

Faurax, Joseph. *Bibliographie Loretaine*. 1913.

———. *L'abbé J. Faurax, ... A Lorette, À Lorette ! ! Le Pape Demande Des Pèlerins. V. Manuscrit De Douai* (1500), Chapelle De Roccapietra ... Cheminée De Rouen ... La Fresque De Iesi ... Et Autres Documents Inédits. Vol. 4. 1911.

Hutchison, William Antony. *Loreto and Nazareth: Two Lectures, Containing the Results of Personal Investigation of the Two Sanctuaries*. London: E. Dillon, 1863.

Kerr, Amabel, and Antonio Grassi. *A Saint of the Oratory, The Life of Blessed Antony Grassi*. London: Burns and Oates, 1901.

Laurent, F. *Peregrinatores Medii Aevi Quatuor*.

Liguori, Alfonso Maria de. "A Short Reply to the Extravagant Reform Attempted by the Abbé Rolli." In *The Glories of Mary*, edited by Bishop Coffin. 1868.

Martorelli, Pietro Valerio. *Teatro Istorico della Santa Casa Nazarena Della B. Vergine Maria e Sua Ammirabile Traslazione in Loreto*. 2 vols. 1732.

Meisterman, Barnabé. *Nouveau Guide de Terre Sainte*. 1907.

Meschler, Maurice. *Life of St. Aloysius Gonzaga, Patron of Christian Youth*. 1911.

Northcote, J. Spencer. *Celebrated Sanctuaries of the Madonna*. 1868.

Paulinus of Nola. *Epistola 31 Ad Severum*.

References

Stanley, Dean. *Sinai and Palestine*. 1856.

Taylor, Thérèse and Thomas Nimmo. *Soeur Thérèse of Lisieux, the Little Flower of Jesus; a New and Complete Translation of L'histoire D'une Âme, with an Account of Some Favours Attributed to the Intercession of Soeur Thérèse*. New York: Kennedy, 1912.

Torsellini, Fr. Horace, S.J. *History of Loreto*. Vol. 1. Paris, 1608.

————. *History of the Holy House*. Rome, 1597.

Ward, Wilfrid. *The Life of John Henry, Cardinal Newman, Based on His Private Journals and Correspondence*. 2 vols., New York: Longmans, Green, 1912.

Sophia Institute

Sophia Institute is a nonprofit institution that seeks to nurture the spiritual, moral, and cultural life of souls and to spread the Gospel of Christ in conformity with the authentic teachings of the Roman Catholic Church.

Sophia Institute Press fulfills this mission by offering translations, reprints, and new publications that afford readers a rich source of the enduring wisdom of mankind.

Sophia Institute also operates two popular online Catholic resources: CrisisMagazine.com and CatholicExchange.com.

Crisis Magazine provides insightful cultural analysis that arms readers with the arguments necessary for navigating the ideological and theological minefields of the day. *Catholic Exchange* provides world news from a Catholic perspective as well as daily devotionals and articles that will help you to grow in holiness and live a life consistent with the teachings of the Church.

In 2013, Sophia Institute launched Sophia Institute for Teachers to renew and rebuild Catholic culture through service to Catholic education. With the goal of nurturing the spiritual, moral, and cultural life of souls, and an abiding respect for the role and work of teachers, we strive to provide materials and programs that are at once enlightening to the mind and ennobling to the heart; faithful and complete, as well as useful and practical.

Sophia Institute gratefully recognizes the Solidarity Association for preserving and encouraging the growth of our apostolate over the course of many years. Without their generous and timely support, this book would not be in your hands.

www.SophiaInstitute.com
www.CatholicExchange.com
www.CrisisMagazine.com
www.SophiaInstituteforTeachers.org

Sophia Institute Press® is a registered trademark of Sophia Institute.
Sophia Institute is a tax-exempt institution as defined by the
Internal Revenue Code, Section 501(c)(3). Tax I.D. 22-2548708.